Early Years Practice

Early Years Practice

For Educators & Teachers

Elaine Hallet

SAGE

Los Angeles | London | New Delhi
Singapore | Washington DC

Los Angeles | London | New Delhi
Singapore | Washington DC

SAGE Publications Ltd
1 Oliver's Yard
55 City Road
London EC1Y 1SP

SAGE Publications Inc.
2455 Teller Road
Thousand Oaks, California 91320

SAGE Publications India Pvt Ltd
B 1/I 1 Mohan Cooperative Industrial Area
Mathura Road
New Delhi 110 044

SAGE Publications Asia-Pacific Pte Ltd
3 Church Street
#10-04 Samsung Hub
Singapore 049483

Editor: Jude Bowen
Assistant editor: George Knowles
Production editor: Tom Bedford
Project manager: Jeanette Graham
Copyeditor: Sharon Cawood
Proofreader: Rosemary Campbell
Indexer: Anne Solomito
Marketing manager: Lorna Patkai
Cover designer: Wendy Scott
Typeset by: C&M Digitals (P) Ltd, Chennai, India
Printed and bound in Great Britain by Ashford
Colour Press Ltd

Library of Congress Control Number: 2015941429

British Library Cataloguing in Publication data

A catalogue record for this book is available from
the British Library

ISBN 978-1-4462-9870-1
ISBN 978-1-4462-9871-8 (pbk)

At SAGE we take sustainability seriously. Most of our products are printed in the UK using FSC papers and boards.
When we print overseas we ensure sustainable papers are used as measured by the PREPS grading system.
We undertake an annual audit to monitor our sustainability.

I dedicate this book to my dear Mum, Barbara Hallet (1924–2013), whose nurturing love and care encouraged me into teaching.

Contents

Acknowledgements

I would like to thank and acknowledge the contribution of the many practitioners, educators, teachers, leaders, lecturers, students, parents, carers and children I have worked with over the years who have provided reflective conversations about theory, pedagogy, provision and practice, influencing my thinking and practice through reflective insights.

Thanks also to the team at SAGE, particularly Jude Bowen, Amy Jarrold and George Knowles, who have again supported my writing, from the initial idea of the book discussed with Jude over a cup of coffee in a London park to its completion. Also, thanks to the peer reviewers, who are unknown to me, and who provided helpful and constructive feedback in the development of the book.

About the Author

Elaine Hallet, PhD, has been involved in educating children, practitioners, educators, teachers and students over a career of 36 years and during this time has developed an understanding of how to nurture, scaffold and support children's and adults' learning and professional practice through meaningful contexts. She has worked as an early years teacher, advisory teacher and leader in a range of schools and nurseries, and as a lecturer and leader with students in further and higher education, teaching on a range of early years initial training, post-qualifying, undergraduate, postgraduate and doctoral programmes and sector-endorsed professional awards in early years and integrated centre leadership.

Elaine's research includes foundation degree graduates' continuing professional development through work-based reflective learning, the development of professional identity and the role of graduate early years leaders in the leadership of learning. She is committed to continuing professional learning for the development of professional practice and to supporting practitioners, educators and teachers on their reflective learning journeys of knowledge, understanding and discovery.

Elaine has recently retired from her role as Lecturer in Early Childhood at the Institute of Education, University College London. With a background in early years education and practice, she is an established author with a special interest in the education of young children and practitioners', educators' and teachers' reflective continuing professional learning.

List of Figures and Tables

Figures

Tables

Part 1
Foundations for Early Years Practice

Introduction

The four chapters in Part 1 provide discussion on the foundations for early years practice, exploring the landscape of policy, provision and pedagogy in early years practice. Each chapter addresses a key theme pertinent to the specialism of early years practice and work with children, families and other professionals. The themes discussed lay a firm foundation for specialist early years practice.

Chapter 1, 'The reflective early years professional', explores reflection, reflective learning and practice for practitioners, educators and teachers within a framework of continuing professional learning and developing early years practice for children and families. Theories about reflection, the process of reflection and the concept of a reflective practitioner are examined. Approaches to engaging in reflective practice and developing self-reflective awareness as part of continuing professional learning and growth for change in practice are discussed.

Chapter 2, 'Understanding children', provides a holistic understanding of children and childhood by exploring the concept of childhood and the evolving nature of childhood in contemporary society. Children's rights, agency and voice, safeguarding and protecting children are considered. The use of observation and reflection for understanding children is included within the discussion.

Chapter 3, 'Early years provision in practice', gives a contextual overview of policy and provision in early years services, examining what provision looks like in practice, through a framework of best practice and quality provision.

Chapter 4, 'Early years education and learning', considers features of early education as a specialist area of educational practice for children's learning. The discussion includes examining how children learn and the curriculum as a framework for learning, pedagogy and practice. A range of curriculum frameworks, pedagogical approaches and practices for children's learning and assessment in national and international contexts are discussed.

These four chapters provide a foundation of knowledge on early years provision, services, pedagogy and practice. Each chapter concludes with reflective consideration about implications for practice. Throughout the chapters, *Stories of practice* provide examples of real-life practice and *Questions for reflection* provide opportunities for reflection on the landscape of early years provision and practice. Suggestions for further reading at the end of each chapter signpost the reader to other resources on the themes and issues discussed.

Chapter 1

The Reflective Early Years Professional

Chapter overview

The importance of reflection, reflective learning and practice for practitioners, educators and teachers is considered within a framework of continuing professional learning and developing early years practice for young children and families. An early years workforce of professionals who are reflective, impacts on the quality of provision and practice for children's learning and development. Theories on reflection, the process of reflection and the concept of a reflective practitioner are explored. Approaches to engaging in reflective practice and developing self-reflective awareness as part of continuing professional learning and growth for change in practice are discussed. There is opportunity for reflective thinking about professional practice.

Continuous professional reflective learning

The importance of continuous professional reflective learning for those working with children and families has been recognized as a contributory factor in developing competent practitioners, educators and teachers. In Tickell's (2011) review of the Early Years Foundation Stage (EYFS), a curriculum for babies and young children from birth to 5 years of age, the important contribution of an experienced, well-trained and supported workforce for children's learning and developmental outcomes was identified. The review encouraged those working with babies and young children to engage in reflective practice by considering the effectiveness of their practice within the curriculum framework of the EYFS.

There is a generally held expectation that an individual will be committed to continuing their professional development throughout their career (Bubb and Earley, 2007). Bubb and Earley argue that continuing professional development (CPD) enables practitioners, educators and teachers to consider their everyday practice in light of related theory, to reflect on, review and modify their practice accordingly, enhancing individuals' specialized knowledge and skills, and to grow personally and professionally in self-confidence and self-knowledge.

The term 'continuing professional development', which refers to continuing education and training, is commonly used within educational contexts. Swim and Isik-Ercan (2013: 182), in using the term 'continuous professional *learning*', identify that when professional development is continuous and ongoing with a specific focus on daily practices, those working with children and families will benefit more. Practitioners develop professional dispositions entwined with their daily practices through continuous professional learning (Swim and Isik-Ercan, 2013). These dispositions are shaped through analysis, reflection and documentation within the socio-cultural context of the settings, schools and children's centres in which they work. Through experience of working with children and families, and continuous and reflective professional learning, professionals develop from their initial training as a novice, emerging as an expert and specialist in early years practice; as someone who is competent and capable, critically reflective, collaborative, a researcher and enquirer, independent and autonomous, and who becomes an early years specialist and leader of practice.

In considering the qualities and attributes of a specialist early years workforce, Moss (2011) envisages an early years workforce with professional qualities of ethical and value-based reflective practice. Being reflective and being a reflective practitioner concern qualities and attributes in a person's behaviour – part of the professional way an early years practitioner works (Paige-Smith and Craft, 2011). Moss (2008: 125) conceptualizes an early childhood workforce of 'democratic reflective practitioners'; practitioners, educators and teachers who are critical thinkers, researchers, co-constructors of meaning, with identity and values, who value participation, diversity and dialogue; rather than childcare technicians who carry out routine tasks without due consideration of professional practice. Reflective practice helps to develop professionals who are democratic and reflective.

Reflective practice

Reflective practice is a vital aspect of working with young children. There is an increasing expectation for those working in the early years sector to reflect on their practice in order to enhance their professional development and to improve and change practice (Paige-Smith and Craft, 2011). Reflective practice is a way to consider how we work with young children, families and other professionals, construct the notion of childhood, respond to children's voices, and develop and respond to new professional and inter-professional relationships (Moss and Petrie, 2002). How we engage reflectively with the evolving early years landscape of government policy helps shape early childhood services, provision and practice for children and families.

Government reviews of early years practice (2010–2013) examined the impact of poverty on children's development (Field review, 2010); the contribution of early intervention to closing the educational gap in children's outcomes (Allen review, 2011); multi-agency provision for safeguarding and protecting children (Munro, 2010); the Early Years Foundation Stage curriculum (EYFS) as a framework for children's learning and assessment (Tickell, 2011); early years education and childcare qualifications (Nutbrown, 2012); and the provision of flexible and affordable childcare (Truss, 2013). Due to these changes within the early years sector, reflective practice in settings, children's centres and schools is becoming more embedded as a key expectation for those involved in working with young children and families (Paige-Smith and Craft, 2011). Professionals with reflective abilities are central to implementing policy in practice; this is being able to consider, reflect on and think about existing practice. What is effective? What is not so effective? Being able to review, modify and develop practice within a landscape of policy and change, with a framework of principles and values of practice in the care and education of babies and young children, is essential. How can I improve or change practice to benefit children? Informed and reflective practitioners are engaged in continuous improvement in practice and in translating government policy initiatives into day-to-day practice with children and families (Hevey and Miller, 2000).

Pollard et al. (2002) explain that the process of reflection within a framework of reflective practice should include:

- a focus on goals
- evidence from practice
- being open-minded and inclusive

- regular dialogue with colleagues
- reflection in context
- an awareness of when to change and when to keep existing practice.

Reflection involves purposefully thinking about an experience with the goal of gaining new insights, ideas and understandings (Schon, 1987). As a critical reflector of practice, this process of thinking and learning can be unnerving – to unpick practice then reconstruct it in a differing form can be destabilizing, yet enlightening for professional learning and reflective practice. Reflective practitioners routinely use their reflective insights, ideas and understandings to recognize similarities between their experiences and the new or unique problems they encounter and to inform their actions in new situations, as this early years educator's story of practice shows.

Story of practice: a reflective educator

Marietta is an early years educator working in a toddler room in a daycare setting. Here, she reflects on her recent appraisal with her manager who described her as being reflective, and on how this helped change her practice. Marietta considered how she had done this and realized that the following three questions helped with her reflective thinking and change in practice when she reviewed the snack-time routine:

- What is happening?
- How is it happening?
- What can change?

What is happening?

Marietta observed that some children did not stay for very long at an activity, sometimes not long enough to fully complete it.

How is it happening?

Adults were interrupting children's concentration, by taking children away from their activity for the snack.

What can change?

A change in snack time from a fixed routine to a flexible routine, where children can go to the snack area when they are ready, would help children engage in their activity learning in a sustained way. The change in routine would make snack time more child-centred, the routine fitting around the child, rather than the child fitting into the routine.

Questions for reflection: reflecting on practice

Think about how you could learn from practice and make an improvement. This may be an aspect of your practice or an aspect of practice you have observed. Use the three questions from the above story of practice as prompts for reflection:

- What is happening?
- How is it happening?
- What can change?

The early years educator in the story of practice above, used questions to critically reflect on her practice. Critical reflection is essential for professional learning experiences to impact on practice (Lehrer, 2013). A reflexive process of learning and development empowers professionals to identify their own problems and solutions as reflective practitioners. In Lehrer's research in Quebec, Canada (2013), participants described empowerment as feeling confident, competent and comfortable professionally, as well as being autonomous and engaged in the reflective process, through the identification of their own problems, needs and solutions, using theoretical and experiential knowledge and developing the desire to learn.

Theoretical approaches

Several theoretical approaches explain the relationship between experience, reflection and learning (Kolb, 1984; Schon, 1983). Kolb's (1984) model of the experimental learning cycle demonstrates his theory that people learn from their experience through the process of:

- *reflection* on the things we do (concrete experiences)
- *experimentation* (action) in similar situations at another time, to gain further experience
- *reflection* again, and so on …

This cyclical process of reflection allows practitioners, educators and teachers to learn from experience (Harrison, 2008). Being reflective and being a reflective practitioner refer to a long-term characteristic of a person's behaviour rather than a cognitive activity – a process of seeing and being (Paige-Smith and Craft, 2011). Reflection is part of the cycle of interpretation and response; this is at the centre of professional action in complex situations (Schon, 1983), which can instigate change in the professional self and in practice.

Schon (1983, 1987) furthers understanding of reflective practice with the concept of the 'reflective practitioner' through his theory of reflective practice. For students and adults to become reflective practitioners, educators and teachers, they should be reflective during and after their initial education and training. The two levels of reflection in Schon's theory of reflective practice are reflection-*in*-action and reflection-*on*-action. Reflection-*in*-action concerns adjustments made as adults work with children and families, thinking on their feet (Turley, 2009). Reflection-*on*-action requires more deep thinking; Turley (2009) describes it as a cognitive post-mortem that occurs after an experience when we stop and consider what has happened. What role did I play? What feelings occurred? What might I learn from it? Both levels of reflection might occur after a critical incident, an error, an observation, a difficult situation or an unexpected result. What can I learn from it? Both forms of reflection enable students and professionals to continually learn from their experiences.

Reflection indirectly shapes future action because it begins an internal dialogue of thinking and doing from which professionals learn to become more skilful (Schon, 1987). The notion of reflection-*for*-action extends Schon's theory (Killion and Todnem, 1991). Reflection-*for*-practice is a process through which novice and expert practitioners can begin to anticipate situations and mentally plan and prepare for situations before being faced with new or unforeseen events. It is not sufficient to reflect-in-practice and to reflect-on-practice, as to reflect-*for*-practice is crucial for professional development and the quality of provision and care (Turley, 2009). The following story of practice demonstrates Schon's theory of reflection.

Story of practice: reflective practice

The first child in this story is unreflective, routinely carrying out a daily task.

During an inspection in an infant school, the Ofsted inspector observed a boy carrying out his daily task of watering the plants in the classroom, which he did every day before he went home. The boy came to the last plant in the classroom, one that did not have any leaves or flowers on, looking remarkably like a stick in a pot:

'Why are you watering that?' asked the inspector.

'Cos I always do', answered the boy.

The second child in this story is reflective; she reflects-*in*-practice and makes adjustments during a routine daily task.

During an inspection in an infant school, the Ofsted inspector observed a girl carrying an egg box of cress seeds growing on cotton wool. The girl carried out her daily task of watering the cress seeds, which she did every day before she went home. The seeds were slowly growing, showing green shoots on top of the cotton wool. She came to the last compartment in the egg box. Looking closely at it, she didn't water it; putting her watering can down, she carefully took out some of the green cress shoots:

'Why aren't you watering the seeds in that compartment?' asked the inspector.

'Cos the seeds need space to grow first, and then I'll water them', answered the girl.

The children's class teacher learnt about these incidents in feedback from the inspector. She considers her response and reflects *on* her practice:

- What has she learnt about the daily routine of asking the children to water the plants in the classroom?
- Is it to save her time? Or do the children learn something by doing the task?
- Why didn't she observe the differences in the way the children watered the plants?
- What has she learnt about the two children?
- Are there other things happening around her in the classroom that she doesn't know about?
- How can she include this daily watering routine more in her classroom practice?
- Is there a need to change practice or is the practice all right as it is?

The following questions for reflection help you consider the level of reflection in your own reflective practice.

Questions for reflection: reflective practice

Identify an example of practice that shows reflection-*in*-practice or reflection-*on*-practice. This may be something you have done or observed a practitioner, educator, teacher or child doing. Write a short paragraph about it, and then share it with a colleague in a reflective conversation, as a form of reflection-on-practice,

(Continued)

(Continued)

a focus for reflective thinking and learning. To frame your questions, use the following words as prompts:

- What?
- Why?
- How?
- Where?
- What if...?
- What would happen if...?

You may want to further your reflective conversation and engage in reflection-*for*-practice:

- What plans and preparation could be made for future practice?
- What strategy for future provision and practice could be made based on your reflective conversation?

Developing reflective practice

The challenge in developing reflective practice is finding the time and space to do it. The following are ways for those working with children and families to engage in reflective practice.

Conversation and dialogue

Providing an opportunity for staff to meet regularly for collaborative reflective dialogue establishes a learning culture in which critical reflection can take place (Siraj-Blatchford and Manni, 2007). Pedagogues working in nurseries in the Reggio Emilia region in northern Italy, close the nursery for an afternoon each week, enabling them to meet and engage in reflective dialogue about children's learning.

Visits

The opportunity to visit another school, setting or children's centre to observe and consider practice with others provides reflective time and space for individuals to review provision and practice in light of the work of others. Teaching schools, as a model for continuing professional learning, provide an opportunity for outstanding nurseries and schools to share practice with others (Pen Green, 2012).

Documentation

In Reggio Emilia nurseries, children's learning is recorded through documentation: a child's drawing, a sculpture constructed by a group of children, photographs of children working, playing, discovering, exploring. Pedagogues use this evidence as a focus for their reflective dialogue about each child's learning.

Journal writing

A journal is a reflective space for thinking, a powerful way of developing reflective practice. Keeping a reflective journal enables the writer to think more deeply about issues, and the writing becomes an internal dialogue (Tsang, 2007). Journal writing has enabled children's centre leaders to 'think through what to do next or to work out how things might be done better' (NCSL, 2008: 7). This personal space is a place where you can record information, write about issues, dilemmas and challenges, and explore feelings about and responses to situations. It may also contain information, cuttings from the internet, magazines and newspapers, annotated with reflective thoughts. The process of reflective writing enables professional learning and development (Bolton, 2014) to be an empowering tool for reflection. A reflective journal is unique to an individual. It is useful at times to look through your journal, as your personal and professional learning journey will be storied, and your progression can be reflected on.

Mentoring

The role of a mentor, who is a more experienced professional, contributes to the development of a less experienced professional's knowledge and understanding, skills and professional practice (Robins, 2006). The facilitative and supportive mentoring relationship between the mentor and mentee provides great potential for reflective practice (Ruch, 2007). New staff members joining a setting, children's centre or school require time to reflect on their practice, to link practice to their understanding of theory and to discuss this with more experienced practitioners. Settings, who do best in supporting new staff, designate an experienced practitioner as a mentor (Nutbrown, 2012).

Critical friends

A critical friend is a trusted and supportive colleague who provides regular and ongoing feedback on practice or study. A critical friend actively listens, questions and challenges your knowledge and practice in a supportive and constructive way (Rawlings, 2008), 'encouraging the reflector to look beyond the superficial and think about their feelings and deeper learning' (Leeson, 2010: 188). Critical friends emerge through friendship and associated trusted relationships.

Study groups

Here, groups of students meet together to share their learning and support each other in their studies and reflective practice, significantly contributing to successful learning (Knight et al., 2006). Graduates of an Early Years Sector-Endorsed Foundation Degree (EYSEFD) value the contribution of their study group of friends through their foundation degree and in further undergraduate study (Hallet, 2013). Study groups are formed through friendship, sustaining and supporting study and learning.

Communities of practice

Early years networks in which practitioners, educators, teachers and childminders meet to share and reflect on practice and research, provide space for reflective dialogue. The concept of a community of practice developed from the work of Lave and Wenger (1991), who identified the social learning process that takes place when people meet with a common interest, share ideas and practices, discuss issues and problem-solve, and develop shared understandings and new practices through reflective dialogue. A community of practice develops over time through participation, demonstrating that learning is not static but an emerging process of reflection for development, improvement and change in professional practice (Hallet, 2013).

A reflective learning environment

In a setting, children's centre, school, or in a study context such as a college or university, the head teacher, setting or centre leader or lecturer should establish a reflective learning environment through a climate of trust and respect, with reflection at the heart of learning. Helping staff or students to construct meaning about theory and practice, develop theory from practice, question practice, critique ideas from academic literature and research, enables the development of professional confidence to articulate knowledge, practice and reflections to others. A reflective and supportive learning environment contributes to personal and professional development (Hallet, 2013), in which there is time and space for critical reflection on theory, research and practice.

Self-reflective awareness

Reflection or mindful practice has been likened to a mirror (Moon, 2006). If you look into a mirror, the same image of yourself appears and is reflected back to the viewer. Many people remain trapped at that one window, looking out every day at the same scene, and do things in the same way. However, when you draw back from the window, turn, walk around and see all the different windows and ways of doing things that await your gaze, opportunities for doing things differently appear (Moon, 2006). Moon's metaphor of reflection as looking in a mirror, highlights the importance of the self in developing reflective practice. Reflection helps practitioners, educators and teachers to become more attuned to their sense of self and to understand how this self fits into a larger context that involves others; reflection helps to shape professional identity (Beauchamp and Thomas, 2009). Looking at your practice through different perspectives helps you become critically reflective. Brookfield (1995) describes these differing perspectives as four lenses: (1) your autobiographical lens, focusing on your emotional responses to your experiences; (2) the lens through which children and families using your provision view you; (3) the feedback lens used by your peers and colleagues and other professionals; and (4) the lens of theory and research (Whitehouse, 2014: 38). Feedback from others can be spoken or written down, and how you receive and respond to feedback can influence the positive or negative impact of feedback on the self. How can you use reflection for professional learning from feedback? In the following questions for reflection, the use of constructive feedback to aid the development of the professional self is considered.

 Questions for reflection: using feedback

Consider some feedback you have received from a work colleague, a tutor or a lecturer. Write it down in a narrative to give the feedback some context:

- Make a list identifying *positive* aspects of the feedback.
- Make a list identifying *negative* aspects of the feedback.
- Make a *Feed Forward* list:

  o What have I learnt?
  o What will I modify or develop from my learning?
  o How will I develop my studies or my work with children and families?

To develop further self-awareness as a student or professional working with children, and to better understand your professional self, try the following activities.

SWOT analysis

SWOT stands for Strengths, Weaknesses, Opportunities and Threats. It is a useful framework to audit your strengths and weaknesses; to identify opportunities to resolve weakness; to develop your strengths; and to reflect on what threats there are to prevent your development (Bedford and Wilson, 2013).

Questions for reflection: SWOT analysis and action planning

Using SWOT analysis, assess your strengths, weaknesses, opportunities and threats in your professional learning or practice:

- If you are a student, consider your professional learning on your course.
- If you work with children, consider your professional practice.

Action planning

This involves a process of review, target setting and planning. In the 'Weaknesses' section of your SWOT analysis, identify an area for development and work this into an individual action plan.

Review

- My area for development is ...
- What knowledge, skills and understanding do I need to develop?

Target setting

- What do I want to learn and achieve?
- How long will it take me? The target can be broken down into achievable steps: short-, medium- and long-term achievable goals.

Planning

- What resources do I need?
- Who can help me?
- Do I need any financial help?

Evaluation and review

- How will I know that I have achieved my target?
- How can outcomes be evaluated?

Critical incident analysis

Deepening reflection occurs through analysis of a critical incident, a new or unfore-seen event happening, like an angry parent in the playground; analysis or unpacking of the incident leads to significant learning and knowledge. Critical analysis of the event is described by Dye (2011: 228) as 'a light bulb moment' of deeper insights. These deeper reflective insights provide productive reflection (Cressey and Boud, 2006) on the basis of what happened previously, and productive reflection leads to interventions in work activity that change provision and practice. The following questions for reflection help with critical reflective analysis of an event.

Questions for reflection: critical incident

- Identify an event you want to critically analyse; you may have been involved in the event or you may have observed it
- Write a narrative describing what happened.
- What did you learn from the event – for example, about yourself, others (children, parents/carers, colleagues, students) and the environment?
- What will you do next time?
- How will you share your learning with others?

Reflective practice for change

Reflection or reflective practice is an agent for change within an organization and for an individual's personal and professional learning and development, enabling them to review, modify and change their professional practice (Siraj and Hallet, 2014). The following questions for reflection help you to consider the influence of reflection on your professional learning and practice.

Questions for reflection: reflection and my practice

- Obtain a large piece of paper, pens, pencils and felt-tipped pens.
- Consider the question: What does reflection and reflective practice mean to me?

(Continued)

(Continued)

- Illustrate your understanding on the paper provided; use drawings and words to represent a narrative about your thinking.
- Once completed, share and talk about your narrative with a friend, work colleague or study buddy.

Implications for practice

The creative reflective cycle could be thought of, like a breath, as a vital exchange of energy that goes on between the children and the adults, as breathing is a continuous cycle made up of a progression of stages. The in-breath is the observation: our reading of the environment and what is happening. The pause between the in- and out-breaths is the revisiting, analyzing and generating of possibilities. The out-breath is our response to the children and the environment of enquiry, our breathing life back into it. This is a continuous cycle that involves a reciprocal exchange between adults and the children.

Aguirre Jones and Elders (2009: 12) liken the process of reflection to breathing; it is part of our biology and way of living. To be reflective as an individual or as a collective group requires time and space within a busy working day. This has implications for practice – if reflection is considered within a framework of continuous professional learning and for developing practice, time and space for reflection within and away from the work context should be integrated into working practices.

Further reading

Level 4

Hallet, E. (2013) *The reflective early years practitioner*. London: Sage.
This book explores how work-based reflective learning and reflective practice support the development of reflective early years practitioners.

Level 5

Hughes, G. (2009) 'Talking to oneself: using autobiographical internal dialogue to critique everyday and professional practice', *Reflective Practice*, 10 (4) 451–63.

An interesting journal article, using a bag as a focus for reflection and critique; unpacking and reflecting on the contents of your own bag introduce the concept of critical reflection in a practical way.

Level 6

Bolton, G. (2014) *Reflective practice: writing and professional development* (4th edn). London: Sage.
This interesting book examines the value and relationship of reflective writing in professional learning.

NCTL Teachers' Standards (Early Years)

Standard 8.6
• Reflect on and evaluate the effectiveness of provision, and shape and support good practice.

Hayes, C., Daly, J., Duncan, M., Gill, R. and Whitehouse, A. (2014) *Developing as a reflective early years professional: a thematic approach*. Northwich: Critical Publishing.
This accessible book discusses key themes within early years provision, with a focus on reflective practice.

Chapter 2

Understanding Children

Chapter overview

Young children are at the centre of early years practice. In this chapter, the discussion develops a holistic understanding of young children through exploring the construct of contemporary early childhood in the twenty-first century and the emerging image of a young child; discussing children's rights, participation and voice for the agency of children and considering safeguarding and protecting children. The use of observation and reflection for understanding children is included within the discussion. There is opportunity for reflective thinking about childhood experiences, and stories of practice help with understanding young children in a holistic way.

Contemporary early childhood

From birth, a human grows through broad developmental stages as a baby, toddler, infant, teenager, adult, and then into middle age and later life. There is a generally accepted understanding that childhood as a specific phase of human development exists and is socially constructed through social interaction rather than being a purely natural phenomenon (Maynard and Powell, 2014). The notion of childhood as a space for freedom, innocence and dependence for children is promoted in the western world (Westwood, 2014). Early childhood as an important phase of growth and development is recognized nationally in England in the Allen, Field, Tickell, Truss and Nutbrown reports (2010–2013) (Willow, 2014) and internationally in the Organisation for Economic Co-operation and Development (OECD) reports, *Starting Strong I* (2001) and *Starting Strong II* (2006). The age span of early childhood varies; in England, the introduction of the Early Years Foundation Stage (EYFS) curriculum in 2008, defined the early years of a young child's life from birth to 5 years of age. Internationally, a wider age span from birth to 6 or 7 years of age defines early childhood in Australia, Wales, Scotland and Europe. Early childhood, or the early years of young children's phase of development, usually refers to the time before a child begins school. In some European countries such as Scandinavia, this is when a child is 7 years old. In England, children start full-time compulsory school in the term they are 5 years old. The terms 'early years' and 'early childhood' are used interchangeably in the UK's national context, but not so internationally where the term 'early childhood' is generally used.

In rethinking early childhood, Jones (2009) poses some questions around understanding childhood as a specific time of life. What are children like? What should childhood spaces be? How should adults treat children? Early childhood is culturally specific; a child's childhood varies and differs from continent to continent, western to eastern hemispheres, country to country, and from urban to rural and war-torn to peaceful contexts. The place and the environment in which they live influence children. Sociologists and anthropologists recognize the influence of children's geographies, the relationships they have with familiar places and spaces and the environment they interact with as key factors in shaping children's lives (Thomas, 2014). A child living in a country at war or in a country at peace will experience different childhoods.

Childhood prior to the twentieth century was seen as a preparation for adulthood. In Victorian times, children were dressed in small versions of adult clothes, like a sailor suit, under the notion that children were 'becoming', growing and developing into adults. In the twenty-first century, childhood is changing due to the impact of social developments such as family structure and technology in a digital age (Prout, 2005). In contemporary early childhood, children should be seen as 'being' (being children) rather than 'becoming' (becoming adults) (Lee, 2001: 45). To understand contemporary childhood, the part played by technology and machines contributes to constructing contemporary childhood within a digital, multi-media age.

In the following story of practice, the changing nature of early childhood over the last 50 years to the present day is shown. I reflect on my own childhood as a young girl growing up in the 1960s and on contemporary childhood in the twenty-first century. I reflect on the geography of childhood, interactions with place, space, environment, play materials and people.

Story of practice: reflecting on childhood

When I think of my childhood in the twentieth century, these words come to mind...

Sunny, happy, carefree, play, fun, indoors, outdoors, sisters, friends, friends' houses. Playing with dolls, dressing paper dolls, the doll's house Dad made for us to play with, going to see the neighbour's very old large doll's house in her cold back bedroom. Riding my blue tricycle and speeding down the road on my red scooter. Going to my sister's friend's house at the bottom of the road and making a theatre in her attic to perform and watch plays we made up. Strutting around in pink, plastic, glittery shoes from the dressing-up box. Swapping things with my friend. Playing marbles and jacks with my sisters. A catch-ball game, throwing and catching a tennis ball against the garage door. Skipping in and out of elastic, finger skipping, skipping ropes and skipping rhymes. Going on picnics, walks, playing in fields, Mum telling me the names of wild flowers, picking flowers, pressing them into a book; paddling in streams, collecting rose petals in a jar of water to make scent; playing board and card games like 'Snap' and 'Monopoly' with my family; learning to sew and knit; doing knitting nancy. The television programmes 'Andy Pandy', 'The Wooden Tops', 'Bill and Ben the Flowerpot Men'; the radio programme 'Listen with Mother'; bedtime stories, learning to read with Enid Blyton books, 'The Missing Necklace' being my favourite story book. Getting a weekly comic to read, like 'Bunty', 'Look and Learn' and 'Jackie'. My childhood had continuous play in indoor and outdoor environments and was a social experience, in playing with my sisters and friends.

I now think about a young child in the present day and view the world that surrounds them: the places and spaces, the environment, play materials and people in their childhood.

When I think of childhood in the twenty-first century, these words come to mind...

Technology, digital play, sound, noise, visual images, television, advertising, consumerism, short, quick, fast, buttons, game consoles, video, ipad, ipod, iphone, tablet, smartphone, plastic, bright primary colours, plastic toys, inside, bedroom, singular. Today's childhood seems to be about indoor and individual digital play. I wonder what implications this has for the personal, social and emotional development of young children.

This story of practice shows that the construction of childhood has changed over time. Childhood, then, can be seen as something that is active, changing and changeable (Jones, 2009). Digital technologies impact on young children's childhood experiences. Childhood in a digital age is conflicting: children are seen as digital experts, navigating a range of technologies expertly, and are positioned as innocent victims of a commercial world of media advertising and commercialization (Marsh, 2014). The changing and evolving nature of childhood is placed within the geography of each child's lived reality. The following questions for reflection enable you to reflect on childhood.

〰️ Questions for reflection: reflecting on childhood

Write a narrative about your own childhood, considering the geography of your childhood, your interactions with places, spaces and the environment, with play materials and people.

Write a narrative about a young child's childhood in the twenty-first century, see the world through a young child's eyes. Talking to a young child about what they like to play with and where they like to play will give you an insight into their world. Consider the geography of their childhood, their interactions with places, spaces and the environment, with play materials and people.

Talk with a member of an older generation: a grandparent, an aunt or uncle; enquire about their childhood experiences. Consider the geography of their childhood, their interactions with places, spaces and the environment, with play materials and people.

Reflect on these childhood experiences in a comparative way:

- How do childhood experiences through the ages help young children to grow and develop in a holistic way?

  o Are there any similarities?
  o Are there any differences?

- Consider your holistic development and today's children's physical, intellectual, language, emotional and social development.

  o Are there any similarities?
  o Are there any differences?

The image of a young child

There are tensions about how society views and constructs images of young children. Are they vulnerable or capable; innocent or sinful; passive or active; fearful and in need of protection; a mini-adult or a child; in need or deserving of rights? Are children seen as dependent on adults or as agents in their own right, capable of views, opinions, decisions, participation and actions on their own behalf? Are children viewed as active participants with a voice in society or as individuals for whom others make decisions? (Jones, 2012).

It is only since 1990 that children have become a subject of study in their own right (Brockliss and Montgomery, 2013). Following the Rumbold report (DES, 1990), which recommended a more highly qualified workforce for improved quality of provision for young children in England, Early Childhood Studies as an academic subject in undergraduate and postgraduate degrees was introduced. As Jones (2009) points out, promoting a multi-disciplinary approach to studying and understanding young children, a holistic approach to the image of the child and the construct of early childhood in contemporary society, is different to the image and construct of a child in Victorian times when children had to 'be seen and not heard'.

In contemporary society, social and cultural aspects influence the current image of the child, which is very different to the Victorian construct. Pictures in story books; language used by adults, such as 'I want a strong boy to carry this chair'; interactions between adults and children – for example, physically passing a baby boy to an adult in a rough way compared with the gentle handling of a baby girl; colour association, such as pink for a girl, blue for a boy; gender-associated toys – for example, girls play with dolls, boys play with cars; images in advertising, films and television programmes (e.g. boys as heroes, girls as princesses) all influence children's gender identity as a girl or boy (Browne, 2004).

In government reviews of provision in England (Tickell, Truss, Nutbrown, 2011–2013), the focus on understanding children's holistic development is emphasized by the inclusion of child development modules in workforce training to inform early years educators' and teachers' provision and practice. The notion of developmental readiness is incorporated within the Truss report (2013) through the introduction of the concept of 'school readiness': young children being ready for learning when they go to school. This developmental readiness for school-led provision (NCTL, 2014) is contributing to the image or construct of a child in England as school-ready for learning, rather than a young child being ready for playful learning. This focus on academic achievement and a product-led provision is culturally different to the process-led early childhood provision of Reggio Emilia. Here, pedagogues working in the nurseries have a different image and construct of the young child, as a child who is competent, strong and creative with a hundred voices to express themselves (Abbott and Nutbrown, 2001). The following questions for reflection enable you to consider your own image of the young child.

Questions for reflection: image of a young child

- What is your image or construct of a young child?

These questions may help you to construct an image of a child:

- o What should a child be like?
- o What attributes should children have?
- o What characteristics should children have?
- o How should children be?

- Draw your image of a young child and add descriptive words.
- Share and reflect on your illustration with a work colleague, student or friend; in a reflective conversation, compare your drawings of a young child, discuss any similarities and differences.

Children's rights, participation and voice

The United Nations Convention on the Rights of the Child (UNCRC) (UN, 1989) developed the view that children are holders of rights and capable of exercising those rights; they have a voice and an entitlement to participation in their lives. The Convention is a set of economic, social, cultural, civil and political rights all children have; these are set out in articles, and governments in Europe agree to include these articles in their national legal framework (Jones and Walker, 2011). The 41 articles that define children's rights concern three broad areas of provision (Jones, 2009):

- provision to ensure children's survival and development (welfare rights)
- protection from abuse and exploitation (welfare rights)
- participation in decision making (liberty rights).

Through this framework of social justice and entitlement, the UNCRC affords children protection and equal status with adults (Westwood, 2014). The Ministry of Justice (2009: 5) defines a right as 'something you should always be able to do, to have, to know, to say or to be protected', and a responsibility as 'something you should do for other people, for society or the environment' (Jones and Walker, 2011 :3).

Children's liberty rights within the UNCRC agenda have raised awareness for children to have a voice and participate in making decisions on aspects of their lives. This rights-based entitlement gives respect to children and, through effective participatory practice, empowers them. How do we enable children's voices to be heard? In many primary schools, children are encouraged to participate in making decisions about school provision, as the following story of practice shows.

Story of practice: giving children a voice

Jamie is a primary school teacher with a class of Year 2 children (aged 7 years). After playtime, the afternoon session would begin in a negative way; he needed to sort out the children's playground quarrels. How were they playing outside? During lunchtime play, Jamie observed the children spending a lot of time running about, bumping into each other, causing quarrels and fights. Why was this behaviour happening? In looking around the tarmacked playground, he noticed that games were marked out in white lines, like hopscotch squares, with a snake to jump along and some tree trunks to climb on. There were no quiet areas for children to sit, talk together, read or draw. The lunchtime supervisors were 'policing' this outdoor play space, rather than encouraging children to play together. It wasn't surprising that both the children and adults were behaving in such a way; the play resources in the playground encouraged only physical play. How could an outdoor play space encourage the children to play cooperatively, help them develop friendships and promote their well-being and health in a positive way?

Jamie asked the children in his class what activities they would like at playtime, posing the question, 'Playtime – how shall we play?' This formed the start of hearing children's views about what they liked doing at playtime. Working in small groups, the children designed the playground they wanted. They created new areas: a literacy corner with a large and wide wooden story chair for children to share stories or to sit and talk; a blackboard nailed on a wall for graffiti, with chalks to draw and write with; a box containing clipboards, paper, pencils and crayons for writing and drawing; a stage with a microphone, a box of hats and clothes for children to dress up, enabling them to sing, perform, dance and act out plays; puppets for children to perform puppet shows; skipping ropes for skipping games; and a parachute for coordination games.

These playtime activities would help the children's play behaviour. Jamie realized this would change the role of lunchtime supervisors, who would become play facilitators, interacting with children in a different, more constructive way. It was important that the lunchtime supervisors were in agreement of the change. Jamie arranged a meeting for the children to present their playground designs to the lunchtime supervisors. He invited the head teacher, as funding would be needed and she held the school budget.

The children's ideas were well received and the class was encouraged to take the ideas further. A small group of children was elected to represent the class; they met with the head teacher and discussed funding. The head teacher gave them a stall at the summer fair, promising to match any amount of money they raised. This inspired the children to make things and bake cakes to raise funds. The children budgeted and bought some playground resources for the newly transformed playground. The children became more engaged at playtime, friendships grew and better relationships developed between the children and the lunchtime supervisors because more cooperative play was taking place. The lunchtime supervisors are now play facilitators, often initiating skipping games for the children. Jamie's afternoon session starts in a more positive way: the children are calmer and often talk about their play activities in the playground.

This story of practice shows how children actively participated in decision making. Children being involved in the process of decision making encourages attributes of citizenship – with citizenship comes responsibilities, rights and expectations of ways of behaving within the social group to which the citizen belongs (Nutbrown, 2011). In our daily work with children in a busy classroom, teachers often say 'just a minute'; 'just be patient'; 'just wait'; 'I'll be with you in a minute'. How do we make each child's voice visible? How do we encourage children to be participants rather than receivers? In the following questions for reflection, consider how you listen to children and hear their voices.

 Questions for reflection: giving children a voice

Reflect on your daily work with children – this may be in an early years setting, a home-based or school context. How do I:

- actively listen to children and hear what they say?
- involve children in making decisions that affect their lives?
- respect children and their rights?
- empower children?

Safeguarding and protecting children

Child protection is part of safeguarding and promoting the welfare of children; it refers to activity undertaken to protect specific children who are suffering or are likely to suffer significant harm or neglect (Reid and Burton, 2014). All agencies and individuals should aim to proactively safeguard and promote the welfare of children so that the need to protect them from harm is reduced (DfE, 2013).

The Laming report (Lord Laming, 2003) on the inquiry into the death of an 8-year-old girl, Victoria Climbié, focused on the inadequacies in the existing legislation and guidelines to protect children from abuse and neglect and the responsibility that professionals in education, health and social services have in protecting and safeguarding children. Similarly, the death of 17-month-old Peter Connelly in 2007 highlighted continuing flaws in the child protection system. A further report by Lord Laming (DCSF, 2009) found that many of the recommendations for multi-agency working in his previous report had not been fully implemented by local authorities (Baldock et al., 2013). The Munro review (2010) outlined ways to improve child protection services and, as a result, intervention now takes place earlier. Decisions made to promote children's welfare, as providing alternative care like fostering and adoption and prosecuting offences against children has been promoted due to more awareness of the need to safeguard children (Platt, 2014 :185). Observing children over time is central to safeguarding and protecting children – a change in behaviour, seeing bruising or cuts can raise suspicions of abuse. Keeping a running record of observations can show patterns of behaviour – for example, a child may be withdrawn each Monday following a sleep-over with an absent parent. Observations provide evidence for concern, reporting and action in the protection of children.

The Common Assessment Framework (CAF) as an initial assessment process used by any front-line children's service professional, to provide an assessment of a child when additional needs are identified, aimed to develop more integrated practice, communication and multi-agency working (Baldock et al., 2013). A lead professional for each child as the point of contact for all agencies has been important in embedding safeguarding and support for children with additional needs within universal service provision.

Understanding children through observation

Observation is an essential skill for adults in understanding babies and young children. Observation is part of daily practice and key to adults planning their support for children's ongoing learning and development throughout their early years. Observation through watching and listening makes children's learning, development and well-being 'visible' (Moylett, 2014). The knowledge and understanding of a baby or child that an adult gains through observation should underpin all the work they do, ensuring the best possible education and care for each individual baby or child. Cortvriend and MacLeod-Brudenell (2004: 273) identify the main reasons for observation:

- to determine if the baby/child is developing according to recognized norms
- to enable the adult to reflect on provision and plan effectively for the baby's/child's continuing education and care

- to share accurate information with parents/carers
- to share accurate information with other education/health/social service professionals, if appropriate.

The observation process begins before birth by health care practitioners who undertake pre-birth medical observations in an ultrasound scan during pregnancy to detect normal or abnormal foetal development. Medical observations take place directly after birth by a midwife, paediatrician, obstetrician or doctor who checks on the baby's development. During the first year of the child's life, a health visitor monitors the child's development and health through screening tests to see whether there are any problems relating to hearing, sight, growth or developmental skills. Once a child attends a setting, the observations continue by health care practitioners and staff in the setting, measuring each child's holistic development; the observations are used for planning activities aimed at consolidating and extending each area of learning and development (Cortvriend and MacLeod-Brudenell, 2004). As appropriate, multi-agency professionals also carry out observations to support children with special educational needs. Observations are used as a tool to discover what children already know and can do in order to build on and extend their abilities, interests and ideas (Luff, 2014a). The range of observation techniques available for use is part of a practitioner, early years educator and teacher's toolbox.

The development of observation skills has been part of the training of nursery nurses and early years educators in England for many years. Participant and non-participant observation skills are developed through knowledge and practice of observation techniques such as writing on sticky notes, ticking criteria on a checklist, writing a narrative, observing a target child, tracking a child's activity over time or during a specific event (time and event sampling), documenting learning (documentation), and recording visual observations using photography and filming. See 'Further reading' at the end of the chapter for more information on observation techniques.

Current observation techniques have been influenced by international practices of recording the process of children's learning from New Zealand and Reggio Emilia in Italy. Documenting children's learning in 'learning stories', through narrative and photographs, promotes positive learning dispositions in accordance with the strands of New Zealand's Te Whariki curriculum (Carr and Lee, 2012). This approach has been adapted by those working in early years contexts in England who record children's 'learning journeys' in a folder which is shared with parents and carers, children and staff to celebrate children's progression and signpost ways for further learning and development (Luff, 2014a). Learning journeys focus on the process of learning rather than on the outcomes of children's learning; they provide a catalyst for reflective conversation between children, parents and carers, educators and teachers.

Reflective observation

Reflection is embedded within the process of observing children as demonstrated in Figure 2.1, Reflective observation cycle. An area of a child's learning, development or behaviour to be investigated through observation is identified, and an appropriate technique chosen to record what is observed. The information collected is reflected on and assessed according to criteria, such as health developmental norms, Developmental Matters statements and Early Learning Goals in the EYFS curriculum, in order to identify children's progress and achievement, and to plan provision for

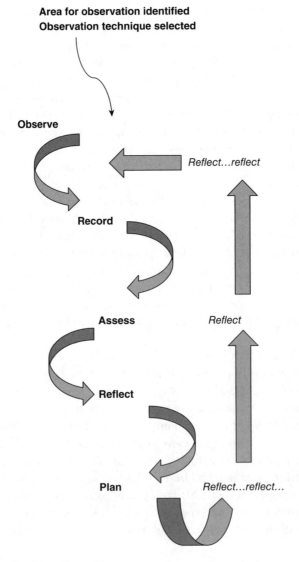

Figure 2.1   Reflective observation cycle

further learning and development. Reflection is threaded through the continuous process of observing children. Reflection informs an understanding of children in a spiral of reflective thinking, learning and review. Space and time for reflective conversation are required. In the Reggio Emilia nurseries, pedagogues designate time when they are not working with children, to use the documentation to reflect on children's learning progression in reflective dialogue.

Recently, documenting observations and reflecting on children's learning have enriched early years practice (Luff, 2014a). The use of digital technology, digital cameras and video recording has enabled children's learning to become visible to children, parents and carers. Observations in digital photographs allow children to see themselves playing and learning, and to talk reflectively about their play and learning with adults and other children, as the following story of practice shows.

Story of practice: reflective observation

Isla is the graduate leader of a nursery and Jenna an early years educator; the two attended a course on pedagogical documentation used in Reggio Emilia nurseries. On return to their setting, at a staff meeting, they discussed observing children through photographic documentation, using photographs to reflect on children's learning progress. The setting had permission from parents and carers to photograph their children. Isla and Jenna were each a key person for a group of children, and they began to digitally photograph children playing and learning. At the end of each day, they reflected on the photographs together, often observing an aspect of a child's learning or play the other had not seen. A slideshow of photographs was projected onto a screen for the children to see at the end of their session. The photos and adults' use of open-ended questions – such as 'Josh, what were you building?', 'Why do you think your building stood up well?' – provided a reflective time and space for children to talk about and review their play and learning. The photographs were displayed daily on an iPad in the entrance for parents and carers to see, and uploaded onto the nursery's webpage so that parents, carers, grandparents and siblings could share the child's play and learning with them at home.

Questions for reflection: reflective observation

For these reflective questions, you will have experience of observing children. If you are an inexperienced observer, try out some of the observation techniques described earlier:

(Continued)

(Continued)

- Use an observation you have carried out:
    - What did you learn about the child you observed?
    - How did information from your observation inform further provision?
    - How did information from your observation inform practice for the child?

In busy early years practice, finding time to reflect on observations to improve provision and practice can be challenging. Consider the following:

- When and how can you designate space and time for reflective conversation with colleagues?
- How can observations be shared with parents/carers?

Implications for practice

'Children are our future' is a phrase commonly used to describe the importance of healthy, educated children for global sustainability. Understanding children underpins working with young children and has implications for practice, particularly in an evolving early years landscape of emerging policy and practice. Within the early years sector, understanding children within the context of contemporary society should inform practitioners', educators' and teachers' work with children and families, putting children at the heart of early years practice.

Further reading

Level 4

Bligh, C., Chambers, S., Davison, C., Lloyd, I., Musgrave, J., O'Sullivan, J. and Waltham, S. (2013) *Well-being in the early years*. Northwich: Critical Publishing. This book promotes a multi-disciplinary approach to the well-being of young children.

Level 5

Jones, P. and Walker, G. (eds) (2011) *Children's rights in practice*. London: Sage. Theoretical issues, key policy developments and good practice concerning children's rights are discussed in this book.

Level 6

Dubiel, J. (2014) *Effective assessment in the Early Years Foundation Stage*. London: Sage.

This book gives in-depth knowledge, understanding and insight on assessment in the EYFS.

NCTL Teachers' Standards (Early Years)

Standard 4.1

- Observe and assess children's development and learning, using this to plan next steps.

Moylett, H. (2014) 'Observing children to improve practice', in T. Maynard and S. Powell (eds) *Early childhood studies* (3rd edn). London: Sage.

The chapter in this book provides examples of observation techniques that can be used in a practical way to observe children.

Standard 7

- Safeguard and promote the welfare of children, and provide a safe learning environment.

Reid, J. and Burton, S. (eds) (2014) *Safeguarding and protecting children in the early years*. Abingdon: Routledge.

This book provides a comprehensive guide to safeguarding and child protection, offering insights into contemporary safeguarding practice.

Chapter 3

Early Years Provision in Practice

Chapter overview

In this chapter, the uniqueness of the early years as a phase of provision is considered. What does early years provision look like in practice? A contextual overview of early years services is given, followed by discussion on key themes underpinning early years services: early intervention, the impact of poverty, closing the educational attainment gap for children, integrated practice, educare and an ethic of care, passion for working with young children, the contribution of a higher educated workforce, the concepts of best practice and quality provision, and ways to measure quality in early years provision and practice. By referring to research, government review and policy, the shaping of the current early years landscape as a foundation for early years provision and practice is discussed. There is opportunity to reflect on early years provision in practice.

Early years services

Early years provision and practice in the UK take place in a range of contexts as services for children and families, publically funded by the local authority, directly by the Department for Education or funded by parents and stakeholders in the private, voluntary or independent sectors. Table 3.1 summarizes types of settings in which service provision for children from birth to 8 years of age takes place.

Table 3.1   Early years provision

Context	Description
Nursery and Nursery school	Provision is delivered in a stand-alone building or separate from the main school building. For children under 5 years.
Nursery class	Provision is delivered in a room located in a school. For children under 5 years.
Reception class	Located in a primary school. The first class a child attends when s/he begins school. For children aged 4–5 years.
Infant school	Provision is delivered in a stand-alone building. For children aged 5–7 years.
Primary school	Provision is delivered in a stand-alone building. For children aged 5–11 years.
Free school	Provision is delivered in a stand-alone building, established by parents. For children aged 5–11 years.
Academy	Provision is delivered in a stand-alone building. For children aged 5–11 years.
Children's centre	Provision is integrated practice carried out by a multi-disciplinary team from health, education and social services. Some children's centres provide a childcare service. For babies and children under 5 years.
Daycare nursery	Provision is a longer day than a school day to wrap care around working parents' employment. For babies and children under 5 years.
Playgroup	Provision is provided through play in locally based buildings, e.g. village hall, church hall. For babies and children under 5 years.
Creche	Sessional daycare for babies and children under 5 years, located in on-site premises to support parental activity, e.g. in a shopping centre as parents go shopping; in a training centre as parents attend training courses. For babies and children under 5 years.
Childminder	Home-based care, with childminders looking after children in their home. For babies and children under 8 years.
Nanny	Home-based care, with a nanny employed by parent(s) to look after their children in their home. For babies and children of any age.
Independent preparatory school (prep school)	Parents pay fees for their children to attend a preparatory school (7–13 years of age) and a pre-prep school for children 3–7 years of age.
Independent school	Children attend an independent school daily or live in the school as boarders. For children up to the age of 18 years.

(Continued)

Table 3.1   (Continued)

Context	Description
Home schooling	Parents teach their children at home, supported by a home tutor. For children and young people of statutory school age.
Breakfast club, after-school club, play scheme	These clubs provide meals and play activities outside the school day. For children aged 5–11 years.
Children and young people's services	Multi-agency provision supporting children, young people and their families through services delivered in various localities, e.g. family support service, speech and language service, autism service.

This rather disparate patchwork of services for children and families is unlike the centrally public-funded daycare in Scandinavian countries, which is a comprehensive and holistic service for children and families (Moss, 2003). Similarly, there are differences in the age children start school. Children in England begin statutory school on a full-time basis in the term in which they are 5 years of age. Many children enter primary school before they reach this compulsory school age, at 4 years old and spend a full year in the reception class. Children in Wales and Scotland begin school in the term after a child's 5th birthday. Therefore, children in the UK begin school aged 4–5 years of age. This is much earlier than other European countries like Austria, Belgium, Denmark, Finland, France, Poland and Sweden, where children begin school when they are 6–7 years old. When children in England are engaging with a fixed curriculum, children in Europe are playing at home or in the kindergarten sandpit (Coughlan, 2008). Is age 5 too young to start formal schooling? The Cambridge Review of Primary Education (Alexander, 2010) found the benefit for children's early starting age is not well supported in research and is open to question. International comparisons of time spent in the classroom and later educational achievement show that Finland is high in performance, yet Finnish children spend least hours in the classroom (Coughlan, 2008).

The range of job titles used by professionals working with young children in nurseries, settings, children's centres and schools in England can cause misconceptions about roles and responsibilities (Adams, 2008), as shown in the list below (adapted from Hallet, 2013: 11):

- childminder
- creche worker
- family support worker
- nanny
- nursery nurse
- early years – educator, practitioner, professional
- early years teacher – with qualified teacher status (QTS), with early years teacher status (EYTS)

- teaching assistant (TA); higher level (HTLA)
- learning mentor, support assistant
- manager – nursery, children's centre
- leader – pre-school, room.

These job titles are different to pedagogue and teacher, which are commonly used in Europe and the Asian Pacific region. The term 'pedagogue' focuses on holistic pedagogy in children's service delivery, while the term 'teacher' concerns educational provision in teaching and learning.

The Truss report, *More great childcare* (2013), addressed the array of job titles used in England, proposing two common terms: 'early years educator' for practitioners qualified to level 3, and 'teacher' for graduates awarded a degree with professional status. Qualified teacher status (QTS) is awarded to graduates working with primary-aged children (5–11 years of age), and early years teacher status (EYTS) is awarded to graduates working in the EYFS with children from birth to 5 years of age; the two are equal in teacher status.

In developing a higher educated workforce, the government introduced the Early Years Initial Teacher Training programme in 2014; those graduates who are leading education and care and who have been judged to meet all of the standards in practice from birth to the end of the EYFS are awarded EYTS (NCTL, 2013). The view that working with young children is regarded as 'women's work' (Taggart, 2011) continues to promote a predominantly female workforce and its lower associated levels of pay (Miller and Cable, 2008). The revised job titles in the Truss review (2013) – 'educator' and 'teacher' – change the role emphasis and status in working with young children from practice as a practitioner to education as an educator, teacher and graduate pedagogical leader. The inequality of pay still remains; true recognized status will only be achieved when the issue of pay in the early years workforce is addressed.

Early intervention

The Centre for Excellence and Outcomes (C4EO, 2010) defines early intervention as a force for transforming the lives of children, families and communities, particularly the most disadvantaged, intervening early to tackle problems emerging for children and families. Early intervention is central to the government's early years policy in England, in believing that every child should have the chance to succeed, regardless of their background (Teather, 2010), and intervening early with troubled families prevents children and their parents falling into a cycle of deprivation and anti-social behaviour.

Giving children 'the best start in life' (C4EO, 2010: 6) by intervening early in a child's life is informed by a greater awareness of the extent to which a child's early development, including before birth, lays the foundations for their future life.

Some health and environmental conditions promote early brain development (C4EO, 2010), and a newborn brain is already shaped by relationships and experiences (Balbernie and Zeedyk, 2010). A baby's brain has a high degree of plasticity and adaptability, therefore forming and reinforcing connections between the brain cells or neurons are key to early brain development.

At the start of their term of office, the Coalition government in England undertook a comprehensive review of early years provision. The Allen review, *Early intervention: the next steps* (2011), found that intervention in the early years of a child's life benefitted children's educational, health and social outcomes more than intervening in a child's later years, as in primary schooling. The Children and Families Bill (DfE, 2013) aims to improve services for vulnerable children and to support strong families in a multi-disciplinary way, in order to close the gap between poverty and educational achievement. C4EO's (2010) research found that identifying risks and resilience factors, using effective interventions and multiple approaches in working with families and service providers, promoted this closing of the gap for children's educational attainment through family support and integrated services.

The impact of poverty on children's lives, identified in the Field review *The foundation years: preventing poor children becoming poor adults* (2010), is a risk factor for young children's health, safety, attainment and positive behaviour, as well as for low birth weight, smoking, disease and infection, injury, neglect and abuse and poor environment (C4EO, 2010). Other risk factors include: poor bonding and attachment, caregiver anxiety and depression, lack of stimulation, inconsistent parenting and lack of aspiration. Resilience factors for children's development include: pre-natal care, childhood immunizations, breastfeeding, good diet, family employment, high aspirations for the child, a mother's education (particularly at degree level), a high-quality home learning environment (HLE) and attending a high-quality pre-school.

To address these risk factors, services need to develop integrated thinking, a shared philosophy and vision, effective communication systems and a shared understanding of roles (Siraj-Blatchford and Manni, 2007). The quality and duration of interventions that combine approaches for both the child and the family close the gap in educational outcomes for young children (Siraj, 2014). Services in Sure Start children's centres bring together services for children, especially those from birth to 5 years, and their families in multi-professional ways, offering children and their families services that integrate health, education, childcare, parental engagement, family support and employment services. Such effective integrated services are improving outcomes for children (Siraj and Hallet, 2012).

The following story of practice shows how a Sure Start children's centre provides a range of services addressing the risk factors described above for children and families.

Story of practice: children's centre services

Our centre provides health, childcare, education and welfare services to support the families in our area. This room is used for mothers to breastfeed their babies and meet with their midwife. The health visitor also uses the room for weighing babies, health screening and giving vaccinations. The room has roof windows, rather than side windows, and subdued light for privacy as a safe place for Muslim mothers to remove their veil if they want to. The next room is a community room for parents to meet in; they can make a cup of tea and sit on the sofas to chat. Every Wednesday, the room is used for advice, for debt counselling and as a job centre. During the week, we have many classes for parents and their children, as you can see from the list of this week's activities:

Stay and play

Parents stay for a while and play with their child; this helps the child settle into their new environment.

Baby massage

Parents learn how to massage their baby to help with bonding and attachment.

Music time

Parents come with their babies and toddlers to make music by playing and shaking instruments, clapping and singing. Eloise, our parent support worker, teaches the parents nursery and finger rhymes to play with their child at home.

Teenage mums' class

A health visitor holds a class for teenage mothers covering parenting knowledge and skills.

Dads' chat

This activity is held in the evening so that fathers can come after work. It is run by our outreach worker, Jake, who is also a dad. It's an informal meeting, usually with bacon sandwiches or sandwiches of some sort! This is a chance for dads to talk together about being a father and looking after children. Jake usually has an activity for them to do, like making a bird box, planting seeds, drumming – something they can do with their child at home.

(Continued)

(Continued)

Eat for health

Children plant and grow vegetables in raised beds in our garden, like lettuce, tomato, potato and marrow. The children pick the produce and, with their parent or carer, who is sometimes a grandparent, make a healthy meal. Jodie, our family support worker, runs the session and has a different recipe each week. The children enjoy eating what they have grown and the parents learn about healthy eating. They also bring their own recipes for others to try. Last week, Hara made some samosas and shared her mother's Indian recipe.

We realize that not all parents are able to come here and take part in the activities in the centre, so our outreach workers take activities out to the community and run them in village, church and school halls and libraries. The children's centre tries to support all children and families as much as possible.

An integrated service is about multi-disciplinary practice, supporting the holistic development of children through 'the team around the child' (Siraj-Blatchford et al., 2007), when health, education, welfare and social care professionals work together. The integration of human service work for young children and their families is a global trend. Policy initiatives in England, Australia, New Zealand and Germany actively support the development of new ways of inter-professional working, giving recognition to features in early years practice evident to those working within the sector (Nolan and Nuttall, 2013). In developing integrated practice, there are barriers, challenges, opportunities, advantages and disadvantages. The following questions for reflection help you to consider these in the context of integrated children's services.

 Questions for reflection: children's services

- barriers
- challenges
- opportunities
- advantages
- disadvantages.

Using the list above, think about what barriers, challenges, opportunities, advantages and disadvantages there are in integrated practice for:

(a) children and families
(b) practitioners.

Consider how these issues can be addressed in integrated practice provision.

Educare and an ethic of care

The concept of 'educare' – the integration of education with care – evolved from the Rumbold report, *Starting with quality* (DES, 1990), which promoted multi-disciplinary provision for the holistic development of children. The term 'Early Childhood Education and Care (ECEC)', commonly used in Europe, refers to all those working in the early years sector who educate and care for children aged birth to 8 years. The close relationship between education and care is specific to working with young children, forming an ethic of care underpinning the work of practitioners, educators and teachers.

This ethic of care concerns promoting, developing and maintaining caring and respectful relationships with children, parents and carers, staff and the multi-professionals guiding professional action (Siraj and Hallet, 2014). Children naturally stimulate emotion and care in adults; parents and carers usually respond to their children in emotionally and caring ways, and there is an expectation that this interaction will continue when their children attend an early years setting (Moyles, 2001). Students in their initial childcare training are expected to develop caring attributes such as sensitivity, warmth and emotionality. Working with young children has physical, intellectual and emotional demands; emotionality within the workplace requires practitioners to manage their feelings and to evoke particular feelings in others. This emotional labour requires high-level thinking, achieved through experience and training (Moyles, 2001). Traditionally, working with young children was viewed as 'women's work', and 'emotional labour' specifically as 'women's way of knowing' (Taggart, 2011: 91). This view has encouraged a predominantly female workforce (Nutbrown, 2012), with few men working with babies and young children. Emotional labour is a sophisticated skill capable of providing practitioners with a sense of empowerment (Osgood, 2011). Those working in the early years sector should embrace emotional labour and the ethic of care as part of their professional identity and emerging professionalism (Osgood, 2006). Emotional professionalism (Osgood, 2010), delivered intuitively by practitioners as well-managed and appropriate emotional practice through daily professional interactions, is what young children need and parents expect.

Passion for working with children

An emotional enthusiasm, a deep and sound commitment, often described as a passion or being passionate, is often expressed by those working with young children, as it brings them close to working with children, families and communities (Moyles, 2001). Passion is a characteristic particularly associated with the early years sector, and linked to the ethic of care concerned with the responsibility of caring for young children (James, 2010). Educare is an area where quality provision and passion are uniquely combined (Osgood, 2006). Passion for working with babies and young children is part of the culture of the early years sector, giving an emotional and affective dimension to working with children and families. Moyles (2006: 86) describes passion as 'a powerful, necessary mindful emotion' that helps educators, teachers and practitioners in their ability to deal in a rational way with a range of events, some of which may constitute a crisis. From my own work with students reflecting on their work with children, this passion is often depicted with the symbol of a heart or the word 'love' (Hallet, 2012). This notion of professional love (Nutbrown and Page, 2008) furthers Moyle's (2006) description of working passionately with young children. I find this interesting and wonder if any other professional group depicts its work in such a way.

Best practice and quality provision

The term 'best practice' is commonly used in the early years sector to denote effective ways found in research and professional practice in delivering services for children and families (Reardon, 2009). The term 'quality' is used to demonstrate a high standard of provision and practice (Sylva et al., 2010). The concept of quality in early childhood education and care has been debated for many years. What does best practice or quality provision for babies and young children look like?

Questions for reflection: a snapshot of best practice

What is best practice in early years provision?

Imagine you are walking around an early years setting: what would you hope to see? Take a snapshot of 'best practice'. Draw images and write key words to describe what you regard as best practice. Share your view with a student or work colleague. Are there any similarities or differences in your views? After your conversation, is there anything you wish to add to your snapshot of best practice?

The judgement of best practice and quality provision involves values: an early years setting may be regarded of high quality to one parent, and of low quality to another parent and similarly to inspectors (Sylva, 2010). Munton et al. (1995) focus on quality indicators rather than on perceptions of quality. They suggest three basic dimensions of quality (Sylva, 2010: 71):

- *structure* – physical facilities and human resources
- *processes* – the education and care processes children experience each day such as conversations with staff
- *outcomes* – the longer-term consequences to individual children of the care and education the child receives.

Using objective, observable and measurable definitions of quality provision in research shows a clear relationship between the quality of early childhood provision and children's developmental outcomes, delivered by a highly educated workforce, as demonstrated in the Effective Provision of Pre-school Education (EPPE) project (Sylva et al., 2004). This six-year longitudinal study of 3,000 children in 141 pre-school settings is the largest European study of the impact of early years education and care on children's developmental outcomes. The research began in 1997, was extended to follow the children to the end of their primary school years, and then further extended to the end of secondary school. The research study is now called the Effective Pre-school, Primary and Secondary Education (EPPSE) project. The EPPSE study finished in 2014, and research findings have contributed to the 'evidence base' for UK policy, significantly informing, influencing and shaping government policy (Pugh, 2010). EPPE's significant impact on policy development in England (Taggart, 2010) is demonstrated in offering universal pre-school provision for young children and families and targeted services in disadvantaged communities.

To assess pre-school quality, the EPPE project focused on the process elements of quality. The main process measurements used were observational rating scales called the Early Childhood Environmental Rating Scale – Extension (ECERS-E) (Sylva et al., 2003). The word environment is used in its broadest sense to include social interactions, pedagogical strategies and relationships between children, and between adults and children. ECERS-E consists of 61 items across 11 sub-scales:

- space and furnishings
- personal care routines
- language – reasoning
- activities
- interaction
- programme structure
- parents and staff

- literacy
- mathematics
- science and the environment
- diversity.

Evidence was collected through mixed methods: all-day observation, interviews with staff and discussion about displays and records available in the setting. Each sub-scale is scored 1–7, with 7 rating 'excellent'. ECERS-E, as an observational instrument, describes the environmental processes of education and care through which children achieve outcomes, more than the physical space and materials on offer (Sylva, 2010: 72–3).

What is the value of pre-school experience for children and does the quality of that experience matter to children? EPPE's research findings showed that pre-school experience compared to none enhances all-round development in children. Disadvantaged children benefit significantly from good quality pre-school experiences, especially when they attend centres with a mixture of children from different social backgrounds. There are differences between individual pre-school settings, with some settings more effective than others in promoting positive child outcomes. Although good quality provision was evident in all types of early years settings, the EPPE project found that quality was higher in settings integrating care and education and in nursery schools (Sammons, 2010). The EPPSE study showed that high-quality pre-schooling is related to better intellectual, social and behavioural development in children. The beneficial effects of pre-school on children's outcomes remained evident in National Curriculum Key Stage 1, particularly in reading and mathematics at the age of 6 years.

There is a growing understanding of the importance of early childhood and later outcomes for children, economically investing in early childhood care and education and the role of a qualified workforce in providing quality provision and practice for children and families (Nutkins et al., 2013). Better-qualified staff teams offer higher quality support for children from 30 months to 5 years of age, in developing communication, language and literacy skills, reasoning, thinking and mathematical skills, as well as better overall curricular quality (Mathers et al., 2011). The EPPE research found higher quality provision and children's cognitive outcomes in pre-schools led by staff with graduate-degree qualifications who were teachers and who supervised less qualified staff (Sylva et al., 2010). Research studies in the USA (Barnett, 2004) investigating the relationship between the education levels of staff and the quality of early years services found that the education levels of staff, together with a specialist professional qualification in Early Childhood Education, predict both the quality of interactions between teacher and child, and children's learning and development. There appears to be a broad consensus that the workforce is central to achieving ambitious policy goals, increasing both the quantity and quality of provision (Urban, 2010). Recent government reviews of early years provision in England (Nutbrown, 2012; Truss, 2013) acknowledge the contribution of graduate early years professionals as leaders of practice and recommend the development of a graduate-led workforce of early years teachers and higher qualified early years educators to level 3 (2013), in raising the quality of provision and practice for children and families.

Implications for practice

At the heart of all that practitioners in the early years do, on a daily basis, is children's development, learning and wellbeing.

Miller's (2010: 5) reflective thought highlights the importance of practitioners', educators' and teachers' early years practice with babies and children. The themes of early intervention, the impact of poverty, closing the educational achievement gap for children, integrated practice, educare, an ethic of care, the contribution of a higher educated workforce, and passion for working with young children, underpin best practice and quality provision for babies and children, laying the foundations for early years practice. As Nolan and Nuttall (2013) point out, working with young children is complex, context specific, culturally located, highly demanding and rich with creative possibilities. Therefore, it is important to sustain these themes in working with children and families; the interaction we have with them makes early years provision and practice unique.

 Further reading

Level 4

Sylva, K., Melhuish, E., Sammons, P., Siraj-Blatchford, I. and Taggart, B. (2010) *Early childhood matters*. Abingdon: Routledge.
This book disseminates findings from the EPPE research project.

Level 5

Osgood, J. (2010) 'Reconstructing professionalism in ECEC: the case for the "critically reflective emotional professional"', 30 (2) 119–33.
In this journal article, the author discusses emotionality in relation to professionalism in the early years sector.

Level 6

Cottle, M. and Alexander, E. (2012) 'Quality in early years settings; government, research and practitioners' perspectives', *British Educational Research Journal*, 38 (4) 635–54.
The research in this journal article considers how practitioners' understandings of 'quality' are influenced by government discourses, personal and professional histories and the context of their setting.

NCTL Teachers' Standards (Early Years)

Standard 8.7
- Understand the importance of and the contribution to multi-agency team working

Nolan, A. and Nuttall, J. (eds) (2013) Special Issue: Integrated children's services: re-thinking research, policy and practice, *Early Years*, 33 (4).
The articles in this journal special issue provide an in-depth understanding of integrated children's services from different international perspectives.

Chapter 4

Early Years Education and Learning

Chapter overview

Early learning is at the centre of early years education; it is a specific phase of education. This chapter discusses founding philosophies, principles of practice, learning theories, dispositions for learning – all exploring how children learn. The curriculum as a framework for practice and learning is considered. A range of curriculum frameworks, pedagogical approaches and practices for children's learning and assessment in national and international contexts are discussed. There is opportunity to reflect on children's early educational experience of learning.

Definitions

Prior to beginning the discussion, some definitions of common terms used in early education are given to aid understanding (Carr, 2001; Gray and Macblain, 2012; Siraj-Blatchford, 2014):

- A *theory* is a set of statements or principles devised to explain a group of facts or phenomena.
- *Learning* is the acquisition of knowledge or skill.
- *Pedagogy* describes the form that teaching takes, the approaches or the processes to learning that are used.
- *Practice* means doing an activity regularly.
- *Curriculum* is all those experiences, activities and events, direct or indirect, intended or otherwise, which occur within an environment designed to foster children's learning and development.
- *Learning dispositions* are an individual's qualities, characteristics and behaviour in contexts where learning takes place.

Principles of early education

The educational component of early years provision has the potential to transform a child's life and set them on a positive learning trajectory for life (Siraj-Blatchford, 2014). Researchers in the Effective Pre-School, Primary and Secondary (EPPSE) study (1997–2014), a longitudinal study on the progress and development of 3,000 children in various pre-school settings, identified a significant long-term, positive cognitive and emotional impact of pre-school education. The children were followed through their primary and secondary education. The quality of early education and care in pre-school continues to influence children's learning life course at every stage of their journey through school; children who go to pre-school are likely to get better General Certificate of Secondary Education (GCSE) results (Siraj-Blatchford, 2014) than those who don't attend pre-school.

Early education is a specific phase of provision and practice that enables young children's learning and development. The principles of early childhood education (ECE) noted by Bruce (1987), and Ball (1994) in his report *Start right*, highlight the importance of early childhood, children's early learning and early education. The authors identify principles of practice underlying ECE that are fundamental to good practice. There are common themes within Bruce (1987) and Ball's (1994) principles of practice:

- *Childhood* is valid in itself and education is part of the present and not just a preparation for adulthood.
- The *whole child* is considered as important.

- *Confident children* who believe in their ability have a head start to learning.
- *Independent children* are those allowed to think for themselves.
- *Learning is linked* and not compartmentalized.
- *Child development* is central to education – there are specific times when children are developmentally receptive to learn, and children develop and learn at different rates.
- *Identifying* what children *can do* is the starting point of education.
- The *people* children interact with and the *relationships* that children form with both children and adults are of central importance.
- *Play and activity* enable children's learning.
- *Play and conversation* are the main ways children learn about themselves, other people and the world around them.
- Children can *initiate* and direct their activity and play.
- *Time and space* are needed by children to produce work of depth and quality.
- The *environment* is important, as early education comprises the interaction between the child and their environment, people and knowledge.

These underlying principles inform professional practice, making ECE a foundation for children to build on as they grow into adulthood. Bruce and Balls' principles of practice, summarized above, from nearly 30 years ago, still apply today. However, with current policy from central government in England promoting school-led provision, these principles of practice need to be upheld robustly by those who educate young children. These principles of practice in the early years have an historical base in influential pioneers and key figures.

Influencers and key figures

Early pioneers and key figures in the history of early childhood education and care influenced thinking and shaped the development of early years pedagogy, provision and practice, and theories about how children learn. The 'founding fathers and mothers' of early years approaches and philosophies (Gray and Macblain, 2012: xiii) in the eighteenth, nineteenth and twentieth centuries, who were philosophers, psychologists and educators, laid the foundation stones for provision and practice that young children experience today. The influential work of J.H. Pestalozzi, Friedrich Froebel, Charlotte Mason, Rachel and Margaret McMillan, Susan Isaacs, Maria Montessori, Jean Piaget, John Bowlby, Lev Vygotsky, Burrhus Frederic Skinner, Elinor Goldschmied, Loris Malaguzzi and Chris Athey helped to establish the importance of young children's holistic learning and development and specialist provision. Table 4.1 summarizes their work and influence on pedagogy, practice, schooling and learning theories.

Table 4.1   Key figures in early childhood education

Key figure	Influences on pedagogy and practice
Friedrich Froebel 1782–1852	His influence informed the fundamental principle of early years practice, that play enables young children's learning and development.
J.H. Pestalozzi 1746–1827	His view on education was that there should be a close connection between the school and the life of the home. He believed that mothers should be educated sufficiently to teach their children at home.
Charlotte Mason 1840–1938	She championed home education and play as being as important as lessons. She was headmistress of one of England's first infant schools.
Rachel McMillan 1859–1917	She established the Rachel McMillan Open Air Nursery School in London with her sister Margaret. She believed that children accessing the outdoors was important for healthy well-being, particularly for children living in the slums. A large garden incorporating shelters and other outdoor facilities was part of her nursery school.
Margaret McMillan 1860–1931	The importance of children being healthy for learning drove her successful campaign for school medical inspections.
Maria Montessori 1870–1952	Montessori's work emphasized the importance of children's learning environments with material that enables children to practise skills for life in a developmental way. To assist children, she designed furniture of a suitable size for them that is seen in practice today.
Susan Isaacs 1885–1948	She established the Malting House School with curricula and pedagogy designed to further the individual development of children.
Elinor Goldschmied 1910–2009	She developed the concept of a 'key person' – an individual member of staff designated to work and care for specific babies and children, liaising with parents/carers to provide continuity of care to lessen anxiety around separation. She also developed play pedagogy for babies and toddlers in the use of treasure baskets and heuristic play.
Loris Malaguzzi 1920–1994	He was founder of the Reggio Emilia approach to pre-school education in Italy which views children as creative and competent, having a hundred languages to express themselves. Children's learning is viewed as a process, documented and shared with parents.
Chris Athey 1924–2011	She identified ways of understanding children's behaviour and learning as 'schemas'.
Key figure	**Theorists and learning theories**
Jean Piaget 1896–1980	A Swiss psychologist who put forward stages of cognitive development in children's early learning.
Lev Vygotsky 1895–1934	A psychologist and educational theorist known for his emphasis on learning as an act of social interaction and his theory of the 'zone of proximal development' (ZPD) in which a child exceeds expectations of learning.
Donald Winnicott 1896–1971	A paediatrician and psychoanalyst who developed environments and practices to enable children to develop emotional security – for example, the use of 'transitional objects' like a cuddly toy for comfort and security in unfamiliar environments.
Burrhus Frederic Skinner 1904–1988	A psychologist who developed a system of learning which involved a stimulus–response approach to modify undesirable behaviour.
John Bowlby 1907–1990	A psychoanalyst renowned for his 'attachment' theory, the mother being a figure of significance and attachment in young children's development.
Jerome Bruner 1951 to present	A psychologist who developed learning theories to understand how children learn – for example, discovery learning, constructivism, the adult's role in 'scaffolding' learning.

Early learning

What all these advocates for children had in common was an understanding of the nature of learning and development in early childhood (Pound, 2014). For adults who work with young children, supporting them in their early years to reach their potential, it is crucial that they understand how children learn and the key role they play in fostering children's lasting ability to becoming effective learners (Stewart, 2011). How children learn is a complex issue. Gray and Macblain (2012: 2) define learning as 'the acquisition of knowledge or skill'. The interplay between *how, what* and *where* children learn is crucial when planning effective learning experiences for young children. Fisher (2008) identifies how young children learn:

- *by being active, learning through first-hand and direct experience.*

Children need opportunities and space to explore and discover:

- *by being independent and motivated.*

Children should be encouraged to take responsibility for their own learning:

- *by talking*, as this is central to the learning process.

Learning should be reciprocal and often initiated and led by the child:

- *by interacting with other children and adults.*

Learning should take place in a social context:

- *by playing.*

Play helps build confidence as children learn to explore, problem solve and relate to others.

The following questions for reflection help you to observe Fisher's aspects of children's learning (summarized) and to reflect on them.

 Questions for reflection: how children learn

Children learn by:

- engaging in and play active learning
- organizing their own learning
- talking with other children or an adult
- interacting with others.

(Continued)

(Continued)

During your work with young children or on your work placement:

- observe how children learn through Fisher's summarized aspects of learning
- write a short narrative about what you observe.

Using your narrative, reflect on what you have learnt about how children learn.

Learning dispositions

Learning dispositions are an individual's qualities, characteristics and behaviour in contexts where learning takes place. Teachers and educators should focus on creating learners; they need to support children's learning dispositions so that children approach activities in ways that allow them to be open to opportunities for learning (Anning and Edwards, 2010) and to become resilient learners, who enjoy learning and feel they are people able to learn.

There is an emphasis on dispositions for learning, which provide the foundations for future independent learning, described as 'habits of mind' and 'patterns of learning' in New Zealand's Te Whariki early childhood curriculum (Anning and Edwards, 2010: 8). Carr (2001) explains that a positive learning disposition is being *ready, willing* and *able* to participate in various ways. Carr's (2001) positive learning dispositions include:

- taking an interest
- being involved
- persisting with difficulty or uncertainty
- communicating with others
- taking responsibility.

In developing effective learners, the teacher's role is crucial, as the teacher takes the child to the next step in a task, by giving some assistance, then gradually withdrawing this assistance so that the child can perform the skill by her- or himself (Carr, 2001). An example of this, demonstrating Bruner's scaffolding learning theory, is a child learning to ride a bike. At first, a child rides a bike with stabilizers, then these are taken off and a parent's hand supports the child's saddle, which is gradually taken away and, finally, the child rides the bike alone and independently. The metaphor of scaffolding, as used in building a house, is used to show how adults facilitate children's learning through guided support.

To encourage positive dispositions to learning, a teacher needs to offer children indoor and outdoor environments with interesting and stimulating experiences to enable them to become successful and effective learners (Feasey and Still, 2010). Some children seem to learn effortlessly, asking and answering questions, understanding new ideas, developing new skills, but there are some children who do not seem to learn so easily, as they face barriers that make learning more difficult – for example, developmental delay, emotional trauma early in life, being hospitalized for a time, receiving limited support from parents/carers, having little or no experience of the English language, or having an additional need (Cowdray, 2013). Children may be from low-income families – poverty affects attainment as early as 22 months of age, and, by their 5th birthday, many of the highest early achieving children from deprived backgrounds will have been overtaken by lower-achieving children from advantaged backgrounds (Collins, 2014). Those working with children in early years settings and schools should be aware of the barriers each child faces and how those barriers might affect their learning and performance (Cowdray, 2013), and should provide differentiated opportunities for learning through various pedagogies and practices.

Pedagogy and practice

The Researching Effective Pedagogy in the Early Years (REPEY) project, undertaken in association with the EPPE project (Siraj-Blatchford and Sylva, 2004), identified the most effective pedagogical strategies used in early years settings to support the development of young children's knowledge, skills and attitudes (at 3–5 years of age).

The REPEY research showed that the most effective pre-school settings, in terms of intellectual, social and dispositional outcomes:

- achieve a balance between opportunities for children that are teacher-initiated group work and child-initiated play activities
- provide curriculum differentiations for cognitive challenge
- value relationships between children
- support children in talking through and resolving conflicts for themselves with the help of an adult
- use open-ended questions and sustained shared thinking (SST).

SST has been described as a 'cognitive dance' (Siraj-Blatchford, 2010a) between two or more individuals who work together, both contributing to the thinking, in developing an extended discourse using questions that have more than one answer – 'what do you think?', 'what would you do?', 'what happens if …?'. SST helps to solve problems, clarify concepts, evaluate activities and extend narratives (Siraj-Blatchford, 2014) – a pedagogical strategy used across the early years curriculum.

Early childhood curriculum

The curriculum as a framework for learning and practice provides the educational structure and direction for teachers and educators to support and develop the educational outcomes and skills of young children (Sylva et al., 1999). The early childhood curriculum is constructed from three different elements that interact with each other:

1. It concerns the *child* who is at the centre of their learning and of processes and structures within the child.
2. It deals with *knowledge* – knowledge the child already has and knowledge the child will acquire competently.
3. It concerns the *environment* which brings the child and knowledge together, appropriately and in a meaningful indoor or outdoor context, using the environment of people, objects or material provision, places and events.

This curriculum framework is illustrated in Figure 4.1, providing a framework for planning, pedagogy and practice for children's early learning.

The key to the early childhood curriculum is for adults to observe, support and extend children's learning. The interaction between the child, the knowledge and

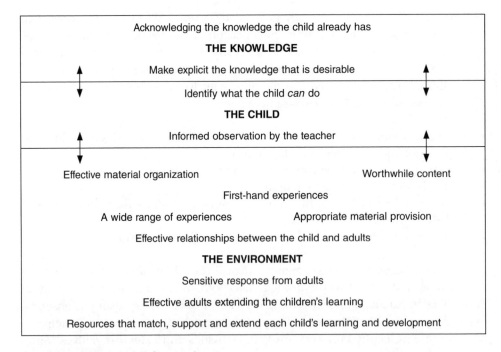

Figure 4.1 The curriculum framework

the environment is fundamental to facilitating children's learning. The environment in which children are taught involves the *people* with whom the child interacts, the *objects* or material provision they encounter, the *way* children are helped to develop skills in using the provision, and the *places and events* experienced. The environment is the mechanism by which the teacher brings the child and different areas of knowledge together (Hallet, 2011).

In the following story of practice, the head teacher, in setting up a new primary school, put learning at the heart of the school, viewing it as a place of learning for the whole community.

Story of practice: a place of learning

Eva is a newly appointed head teacher, tasked with establishing a nursery and primary school for children aged 3–11 years. She views learning as a continuous process throughout life. She wants to create a building central to the local community it serves: a place where learning takes place for the young, for older persons, for families, with continuous professional learning for those who work there, and where learning is taken out into the community. To reflect this philosophy, she calls the school 'High View *Place of Learning*', rather than 'High View *School*', the name promoting a new concept for a school and prompting discussion in the local community. Why is it called a place of learning, rather than a school? I know what a school is; we all went to one. What is different about a place of learning?

 ## Questions for reflection: place of learning

Consider your own values and beliefs about learning. If you opened a new school:

- How do you view learning?
- How would you make learning visible to children, staff, parents/carers and the local community the school serves?

Curriculum frameworks

Principles of practice, pedagogy, values and beliefs about education inform a head teacher's, or nursery or playgroup leader's view of the nursery or school curriculum. Curriculum frameworks for learning are set within a specific social and cultural context, and have a strong influence on the way that programmes and practices are implemented and shaped within early years settings and schools (Ang, 2014). From a socio-cultural approach to pedagogy, Rogers (2014) recognizes children's agency as central to pedagogic relations between adults, babies and young children. The child is central to the curriculum, which should fit around and support the child, rather than the child having to fit into the curriculum. Nationally prescribed curriculum frameworks provide consistency in provision for all early years settings and schools. How society views both the child and childhood is significant in pedagogy and practice in terms of designing and delivering a curriculum. Curricula from national and international contexts are now discussed, highlighting social and cultural influences.

Curricula in the United Kingdom

The four countries of England, Scotland, Wales and Northern Ireland comprise the United Kingdom; each has differing curricula for children. In England, the Early Years Foundation Stage (EYFS) curriculum for babies and children from birth to 5 years of age supports the socio-cultural view that children develop in a progressive developmental way, through ages and stages of development. The learning and development requirements in the EYFS curriculum comprise Early Learning Goals that summarize the knowledge, skills and understanding that all children should have gained by the end of their reception year. At the end of the EYFS, in the final term in which a child becomes 5 years old, each child's progress is assessed against expected levels of attainment and their readiness for Year 1 and the start of statutory school (DfE, 2014a). This Early Years Foundation Stage Profile (EYFSP) forms the baseline assessment for a child starting school.

Four guiding principles in the EYFS should develop practice, every child is unique, they learn through positive relationships, in enabling environments and in different ways and at different rates (DfE, 2014a). Interconnected Prime and Specific Areas of Learning shape educational programmes in early years settings and schools and provide bodies of knowledge for children to learn. There are three Prime Areas of Learning:

- communication and language
- physical development
- personal, social and emotional development.

There are four Specific Areas of Learning:

- literacy
- mathematics

- understanding the world
- expressive arts and design.

The National Curriculum (NC) follows the EYFS curriculum through primary and secondary education (5–16 years of age). The NC provides pupils with essential knowledge to be educated citizens and prepares them for responsibilities and experiences in later life (DfE, 2014b). Programmes of study, Core subjects (English, Mathematics, Science) and Foundation subjects (Art and Design, Computing, Design and Technology, Geography, History, Music and Physical Education) form the body of knowledge within the curriculum. A developmental approach to learning continues in four Key Stages of learning and assessment, and children are assessed at the end of each Key Stage. Key Stage 1 in the Primary National Curriculum follows the EYFS and is for children aged 5–7 years. The change in pedagogy from a play-based EYFS curriculum to a more formal and structured learning pedagogy in NC Key Stage 1, is problematic for a smooth transition to school (Brooker et al., 2010). In the drive for school readiness, pedagogical continuity is an issue to be addressed.

The Education Scotland (2012) strategy, *Transforming Lives through Learning*, recognizes that learning begins at birth and continues throughout life, that is, learning is lifelong, and aims to help learners develop the skills they need for learning, life and work. The two interconnecting curriculum frameworks, *Transforming Lives through Learning* and *Pre-Birth to Three: Positive Outcomes for Scotland's Children and Families*, recognize the importance of pregnancy and the first three years in children's holistic development and the impact of influences on children's cognitive development throughout their lives. Four key principles inform the interaction of those who work with babies and young children:

- rights of the child
- relationships
- responsive care
- respect.

The Curriculum for Excellence for children and young people aged 3–18 years builds on the Pre-Birth to Three curriculum. The curriculum aims to ensure that all children and young people develop the knowledge, skills and attributes they need to flourish in life, learning and work to become a successful learner, a confident individual, a responsible citizen and an effective communicator.

In Wales, an education and learning continuum underpins the National Curriculum for children and young people aged 3–19 years. Part of this curriculum is a framework for children's learning for 3–7-year-olds, with the Foundation Phase based on the principle that early years provision should offer a sound foundation for future learning through a developmentally appropriate curriculum. In the Areas of Learning in the curriculum framework, each educational programme sets out what a child should be taught, along with their expected outcomes:

- personal and social development, well-being and cultural diversity
- language, literacy and communication skills
- mathematical development
- Welsh language development
- knowledge and understanding of the world
- physical development
- creative development.

The Foundation Phase curriculum in Wales focuses on learning from experience and active involvement, developing each child holistically and as an individual.

The Foundation Stage (FS) curriculum uses play as a context for learning, recognizing that play is an important factor in the social, emotional and educational development of the child. The curriculum spans three stages of the primary curriculum: Foundation Stage and Primary Years 1 and 2. The FS curriculum starts for children when they begin compulsory schooling at 4 years old and continues through three Key Stages in primary and secondary schooling, up to when children leave school at 16 years of age. The FS has six areas of learning:

- language and literacy
- mathematics and numeracy
- the arts
- the world around us
- personal development and mutual understanding
- physical development and movement.

Curriculum and pedagogy from international contexts

Curriculum and pedagogy from international contexts have influenced pedagogy, practice and assessment in early years education in the UK. Te Whariki is the early childhood curriculum for children under 5 years of age in New Zealand – a holistic curriculum that integrates education and care. A bicultural vision of early childhood underpins the curriculum framework, reflecting the cultural diversity of the Maori and New Zealand populations. The curriculum emphasizes learning partnerships between teachers and parents; viewed as resources for learning, the curriculum empowers the child to access these resources for learning.

'Whariki' means 'mat', the ethos behind Te Whariki being that every child has a curriculum mat fitting her or his needs, culture and personality. Teachers weave a holistic curriculum in response to children's learning and development in the early childhood setting and the wider context of the child's world. The Te Whariki framework has four *curriculum principles* (empowerment, holistic development, family and community, relationships) and five strands of *aspirations for children* (well-being, belonging, contributing, communicating, exploring). The five strands represent learning – while other strands are individually defined and added, the strands are woven through the four curriculum principles, making the curriculum for every child unique and appropriate (Lee et al., 2013).

Assessment in the Te Whariki curriculum is based on narrative, using story to record the process of children's learning, rather than measuring and quantifying learning by goals and levels, as in the EYFS curriculum. Assessments written as stories are known as 'learning stories' (Carr, 2001), demonstrating that children's learning is continuously happening and not a discontinuous activity (Drummond, 2008). A learning story describes a significant learning event and gives analysis of learning through questioning – 'What have I learnt about Cillian's learning today? What learning do I think was happening?' Opportunities and possibilities provide guidance for planning future learning.

As an approach to assessment, learning stories have led to a better understanding of how children learn: 'Learning stories now capture the magic of children as they discover the world in a way more formal assessments could never do' (Waugh, 2013: 108). This approach to assessment is used in some early years settings, including photographs in children's learning stories, which provide real-life snapshots of learning to share with parents and carers.

The pedagogy used in Reggio Emilia infant-toddler centres and nurseries regards early childhood education not as a curriculum but as a philosophical and pedagogical, child-centred approach to teaching and learning based around the image of a child who is rich in potential, strong, powerful and competent, a capable learner, with agency, the ability to question and to actively participate in the co-construction of knowledge and culture. Children are viewed as curious and creative beings with multiple ways of expressing themselves, through a 'hundred languages' (Cox, 2014: 101). Respectful listening and relationships between children, parents, pedagogues and the environment are central to this pedagogy. The environment is regarded as the third teacher, bringing together a creative, child-centred pedagogy to young children's learning and development.

Documenting children's learning is embedded in Reggio Emilia pedagogy. Pedagogues document children's learning progression though photographs, narrative and discussion, where pedagogues discuss how each child is learning. Rather than an end product, like a child's painting displayed on a classroom wall, the process of learning is at the centre of assessment practice in Reggio Emilia settings. Pedagogical documentation in the early years aims to make visible children's learning processes during learning activities. This assessment practice, defined as process documentation (Picchio et al., 2014), has influenced some assessment practices in early years educational contexts. A progress meeting in some primary schools, in which children's progress is discussed between a class teacher and their head teacher, gives children's learning as a focus for discussion. Although attainment targets may be used as a benchmark to frame the discussion, children's learning progression is part of reflective educational dialogue.

The introduction of continuous indoor and outdoor provision in the EYFS curriculum (DfES, 2007) promoted the development of outdoor space for play and learning. This statutory requirement helped develop outdoor provision for learning that had been overlooked, particularly for reception and Year 1 classes (4- and 5-year-olds). The use of outdoor space for children's learning includes visits to natural and wild environments, and play in outdoor spaces within a setting and in forest schools (Waller, 2009).

Pedagogy for outdoor learning in the UK has been influenced by forest school pedagogy and practice in Scandinavia. The forest or woodland is the outdoor classroom, with a child-led curriculum supporting children's well-being and healthy learning (Knight, 2009). The forest or woodland becomes a space for children to playfully explore, set their own agenda for learning and develop holistically (Blackwell and Pound, 2011). Many schools and early years settings have a woodland area as an outdoor learning space.

Curriculum and pedagogy are socio-culturally specific and, therefore, cannot be transported wholesale to other cultural settings (Maynard and Chicken, 2012). The international practices discussed have influenced practice. Teachers' and educators' understanding of children's learning has developed through an awareness of learning dispositions and the recording of children's learning in learning stories from New Zealand's Te Whariki curriculum and the work of Margaret Carr. From study visits to infant-toddler centres and nurseries in Reggio Emilia, creative, child-led pedagogy and the documenting of children's learning have influenced pedagogy and practice (Hallet, 2014). Forest school pedagogy in Scandinavia has influenced provision for outdoor learning. Teachers have adapted these educational philosophies, pedagogies and practices from Australasia and Europe by developing their professional knowledge, pedagogy and practice.

Implications for practice

Children are affected by the context in which learning takes place, the people involved in the process, and the values and beliefs that are embedded in it.

This statement (DES, 1990: Para. 67) encapsulates children's learning within early years education. Educators and teachers involved in educating children are required at times to articulate pedagogy, values and beliefs underpinning their practice to parents, inspectors and others. Having sound knowledge and understanding of pedagogy, curricula and practice affects the quality of educational provision. It is important that those providing children's early education have knowledge and understanding about how children learn through developmentally appropriate pedagogy and practice for children's learning and educational achievement.

 Further reading

Level 4

Ang, L. (ed.) (2014) *The early years curriculum: the UK context and beyond.* Abingdon: Routledge.
Each chapter in this book examines a curriculum model from a different country.

Level 5

Lee, W., Carr, M., Soutar, B. and Mitchell, L. (2013) *Understanding the Te Whariki approach*. Abingdon: Routledge.
This book discusses the Te Whariki curriculum and learning stories as an assessment practice.

Level 6

Basford, J. and Bath, C. (2014) 'Playing the assessment game: an English early childhood education perspective', *Early Years*, 34 (2) 119–32.
This journal article discusses assessment in the EYFS curriculum.

NCTL Teachers' Standards (Early Years)

Standard 2.2
- Demonstrate knowledge and understanding of how babies and children learn and develop.

Gray, C. and MacBlain, S. (2015) *Learning theories in early childhood* (2nd edn). London: Sage.
This book discusses early philosophies, approaches to children's learning and key learning theories.

Part 2
Early Years Education

Introduction

The four chapters in Part 2 discuss pedagogy, provision and practice in early years education. Children's learning through play is central to early years practice, and the notion of playful early years education is explored. The first chapter considers the concept of play and children learning in a playful way; subsequently, play is referred to throughout Part 2. The following three chapters consider an area of children's learning, examining pedagogy and practice in early years education and early years curricula as a framework for educational learning.

In Chapter 5, 'Playful learning', play as pedagogy for children's playful learning and play-based practice are explored. Childhood play, theories of play, play in early years education and the role of adults in facilitating play within indoor and outdoor contexts, are discussed.

Chapter 6, 'Early language and literacy', examines children's language and literacy learning as an essential life skill for communicating through spoken and written symbols. Pedagogical practices for language development and early reading and writing in settings, at school and at home are discussed, including using environmental print and literacy events for meaningful, real-life literacy interactions.

Chapter 7, 'Creative children', explores the development of children's creativity and creative thinking. Creative pedagogy and practices which enable children's creativity and creative learning, like possibility thinking and sustained shared thinking, are considered.

Chapter 8, 'Children exploring', considers children's exploratory and investigative learning for developing knowledge and understanding of the world in which they live. Pedagogy and practices that create enabling indoor and outdoor environments for children to explore, for mathematical and scientific knowledge, understanding and development of skills, are considered.

Throughout these chapters, the role of the practitioner, educator and teacher in facilitating early learning through enabling early years educational practice, is considered. Each chapter concludes with a reflective consideration of implications for practice. *Stories of practice* provide examples of real-life practice, while *Questions for reflection* provide opportunities for reflection on early years education. Suggestions for further reading at the end of each chapter signpost the reader to other resources to read on the themes and issues discussed.

Chapter 5
Playful Learning

Chapter overview

This chapter examines play as pedagogy for playful learning for children's holistic development and play-based practice. The concept of play is explored by examining play in early childhood, play behaviours, types of play, the concept of playfulness, theories of play, the role of play as playful pedagogy for learning in early years education, policy and play practices. The adult's role in facilitating playful contexts for children's learning is discussed. There is opportunity for reflecting on childhood play experiences and contexts in which playful learning takes place.

Pedagogy for play-based practice

There is a long tradition of play-based practice in early years education (Moyles, 2010a) as valued pedagogy for children's holistic learning and development. The word 'play' is used in early years policies and documents (Moyles, 2010b) and in relation to children's behaviour. The concept of play has multiple meanings and understandings for practitioners, teachers, educators and policy makers (Moyles, 2010b). Although play is a central pedagogy in early years practice, particularly for children from birth to 5 years of age, there is a tension between the division of work and play in some early years classrooms for older children, from when they start school at 5 years of age (Rogers, 2011) and throughout their primary schooling to 11 years of age in England. The view of the teacher – 'you can play when you've finished your work' – lessens the value of play in relation to teacher-directed work for children, with play used as a reward rather than a pedagogical practice for learning. This division of play and work may prevent the integration of play into pedagogical practice (Rogers, 2011). New pedagogies of play require a reconceptualization of play and the connections between play, teaching and learning should be strengthened (Dockett, 2011). For teachers and educators, being an advocate for play within a predominantly school-led education system is a challenge; Dockett (2011) argues that they need a comprehensive understanding of play grounded in research and practice that reflect the relevant social and cultural contexts of the children they work with.

What does play look like? Moyles (2010a: 24–5) helps to define children's play as a child-centred, process-led activity:

- Play is intrinsically motivated and self-initiated.
- The play process is more important than what it produces.
- Everything is possible in play – reality can be disregarded and imagination allowed to take over.
- Play is highly creative and flexible.
- Play is free from externally applied 'rules'.
- Play involves the active participation of both mind and body.
- Play has positive, often pleasurable, effects on the player(s).
- The context of play is open-ended.
- The player is deeply involved and committed.
- The player has a real sense of decision making, ownership and control over the play.
- The player is self-directed and play is often self-initiated.

Play is part of childhood

Play is an activity shared by humans and animals alike and is something most people engage in (Moyles, 2010c). Play is associated with children, but teenagers and adults also engage in playful activity – snowball fights take place on cold, crisp winter days; during a trip to the park, the children play on the swings, but on the way their aunt may playfully swish up the autumn leaves as she walks with the children; their uncle may engage in rough-and-tumble play up and down a grassy bank, just as a pair of cubs may play-fight on the African plain. Play is part of childhood, embedded within a child's world: their home, indoor and outdoor spaces, the neighbourhood, culture, siblings, friends and significant adults are play resources and contexts for playful learning. Reflecting on your childhood play experiences develops in you an understanding of the notion of play through the eyes of a child.

 Questions for reflection: my childhood play

Reflect on your childhood play experiences. The following questions will prompt your memory and reflection; write down a few notes in response. With a talk partner, friend, sibling or work colleague, share your experiences in a reflective conversation:

- *What* was your favourite toy or game?
- *Where* did you play?
- *When* did you play?
- *Who* did you play with?
- *Were* any adults involved in your play?

Following your conversation, write down key words that describe your childhood play experiences, and discuss similarities and differences with your talk partner.

Your childhood play probably included many free-flow play experiences that were initiated by you or other children, were open-ended, were not time restricted, were culture and context specific. As a playful child, you were approaching activities and experiences with the 'mood or spirit of play', using playful ways of interacting with others, with the environment and the materials and resources within it; this may have included using humour, teasing, jokes, mimicry, riddles, rhymes, singing and chanting, and clapping games. Playful moods range from boisterous, wild, dizzy and risky play to quiet, focused contemplation. Play and playfulness are integral to the ways humans learn and interact across generations, cultures and contexts (Wood, 2010). Bruce's 'Twelve Features of Play' (2005: 132) illustrate children's playful behaviours:

1. Children use first-hand, direct experience.
2. Children make up rules as they go along.
3. Children symbolically represent in their play, making play props.

4. Children choose to play; they cannot be made to play.
5. Children rehearse possible futures in their role-play.
6. Children pretend when they play.
7. Children sometimes play alone.
8. Children play together as companions or cooperatively in pairs or groups.
9. There will be a play agenda for each person playing. If adults join in, their play agendas will be more important than those of the children.
10. Children at play will be deeply involved and difficult to distract from their deep learning. Children 'wallow in their play'.
11. Children try out their most recent learning, skills and competences when they play. They seem to celebrate what they know.
12. Children at play coordinate their ideas and feelings and make sense of their relationships and culture. When play is coordinated, it flows along in a sustained way; this is called free-flow play.

There are many terms used for types of play: imaginary play, role-play, pretend play, socio-dramatic play, symbolic play, creative play, messy play, exploratory play, physical play, risky play, rough-and-tumble play, adventurous play, superhero play, outdoor play, structured play; these all illicit different play behaviours. Playful pedagogy supports babies, toddlers, infants and primary-aged children's learning and development. Young children's preoccupation with role-play is widely recognized: children aged 3–5 years engage in it more than any other type of play (Rogers and Evans, 2008). Role-play permeates all types of play, helping children develop social competence, explore language and understand the world around them.

Role-play

Role-play that encompasses many types of play is visible in early years settings and in home contexts. Play props and planned contexts enable role-play: children using a length of material from the dressing-up box as a cape for their superhero character; toddlers tying two cardboard boxes together as a train; children playing 'mummies and daddies' in the home corner; children being customer and shop-keeper in a makeshift shop; being waitress and customer in a café; creating a fantasy land of sweets in the sand tray with pebbles, shells and twigs, or telling an adventure story through voices of the small-world figures that live there.

Role-play is defined by Harris (2000: 30) as 'shared pretend play between children in which they temporarily act out the part of someone else using pretend actions and utterances'. Children's individual, active participation and involvement in situated social contexts and practices create highly effective learning situations in which the social construction of knowledge takes place through joint activity where children are guided by adults or more competent peers (Rogers and Evans, 2008).

Role-play provides power, agency, transformation and control for children (Hall, 2010), helping them to understand others and their future roles in society, and develop social interactions and cultural understanding. As the predominantly preferred activity of social engagement in young children, role-play provides an ideal context in which children can develop social competence and a sense of well-being, providing opportunities for the resolution of conflict in authentic situations (Rogers and Evans, 2008). The following story of practice illustrates the control and agency a child has in their transformed imaginary world, where reality is suspended for a short while (Rogers and Evans, 2008, adapted).

Story of practice – sssh baby's asleep

It was Christmas time; there was a stable in the corner of the reception classroom. Elespeth, aged 4, took my hand and led me into the stable for the first time. 'Sssh the baby's asleep', she said. We tiptoed to the manger made out of a cardboard box trimmed with gold tinsel and saw a 'Jesus' asleep on the hay. Mary and Joseph were sitting by the manger along with two shepherds, Santa and some soft toys (a reindeer, a lamb and a donkey). We stood looking at the baby and at the Christmas scene the children had created. Elespeth then pulled my hand and said, 'Baby's waking up now ... let's go.' We tiptoed and quietly left this imaginary world and stepped back into the reality of the reception classroom.

Babies and toddlers have an enthusiasm for physical play, they are curious, always on the move, exploring the world around them, reaching for things with their whole bodies. Physical play helps them to control their bodies, to grow in mobility, agility, dexterity and to foster independence (Manning-Morton and Thorp, 2010). For very young children, role-play is part of their physical play, as the following story of practice shows, via a toddler's physical and role-play experience in an outdoor space.

Story of practice: being a gardener

Josh, aged 21 months, is playing in his childminder's garden. He is pretending to be a gardener, pushing a small wheelbarrow loaded with stones, leaves and soft toys in a self-chosen circuit around the garden. This includes navigating around bushes and between the sandpit and the garden wall. Occasionally, he stops to pick up a fallen toy, re-load his wheelbarrow and continue pushing. His circuits around the garden get quicker as his confidence and familiarity with the garden increase.

Questions for reflection: role-play

Observe a child engaged in role-play activity and write a narrative of what you see, using the following questions:

- What is the context in which the play takes place – is it the home, pre-school, nursery, school? Is it indoors or outdoors?
- Is the child playing alone or together with others?
- Is it child-initiated play or planned and adult-directed play?
- What is the child you observe doing?
- What role is the child playing?
- Is the child using any play props?
- Throughout the role-play, are there any other types of play you observe?

Reflect on the statements about the value of role-play in children's social and emotional development, referring to your observation of role-play:

- How does the role-play activity develop the child's agency?
- How does the role-play activity develop the child's social competence?
- How does the role-play activity develop the child's well-being?
- Does the role-play activity provide opportunity for resolution of conflict?
- Does the role-play activity help the child understand future roles in society?
- Comment on any other aspects of the role-play observed that interest you.

Theories for understanding play

Theories of play show how play was viewed by society, developed over centuries to help our understanding of play. Theories of play in the 1930s to 1960s were child-centred and emphasized the pleasure of playing. The activity of play, viewed as a source of pleasure for children, was not dependent on anticipated results. Freud believed play to be a cathartic experience, helping children to cope with emotions such as anxiety and conflict. Winnicott valued play in the development of attachments and relationships. The importance of a transitional object like a blanket or teddy can represent a relationship like an imaginary friend or can help in the transition from a familiar home context to an unfamiliar nursery environment. In his child-centred theory of play, Piaget placed importance on the environment. Through play, children interact with and explore their environment;

they unify experiences, knowledge and understanding. Spencer developed an excess energy theory of play, comparing industrial machinery that lets off steam, to children who play to let off surplus energy. This theory-in-practice can be seen in playtime when children are 'let out' into the school playground to run about, letting off surplus energy.

In the 1970s, 1980s and 1990s, two contrasting theories of play emerged, developed by Bruner, Hutts, Tizards and Groos. First, play was viewed as a preparation for life. Play as part of education prepares children for future life; it initiates children into what they need to do in the future. Adults structure play situations, to guide play and the learning that takes place. A water tray with ladles, tubes and cups facilitates playful learning, for mathematical understanding of capacity. A home corner enables children to role-play future parenting roles. Newspapers, magazines, comics, calendars, notebook and pencil, recipe books provide opportunities for early writing and reading.

Second, the theory views play as an integrating mechanism, enabling children to sort out their ideas, to know themselves, to experience, control, innovate, create, imagine and demonstrate their uniqueness. Bruce's (2001) notion of free-flow play as child-initiated activity without adults leading in this play but acting as sensitive catalysts in children's play development, demonstrates this theory. As play facilitators, adults provide provocations, resources or play props. A box with coloured lengths of material, hats and handbags inside – What shall I wear? Who shall I become? A teddy bear is found in the playground – who does she belong to? How will she get home? A basket of cutlery, shakers, sieves and pebbles – what sound can I make? A small woodland area – it's going to rain, so how can we make a shelter? A large box tied up with silver ribbon with the label 'Please open me' is left on a table in the classroom – Who left it? What is inside? Who should open it?

The adult's role in play

The adult's role in play is to facilitate, resource, support, extend, enhance, respond, play alongside and play with children, remembering that babies and young children often have play agendas that may not be explicit to adults (Hallet and Cortvriend, 2008). Play starts in the home, with parents and carers, a child's extended family and siblings. Babies, toddlers and children need spontaneous playful interactions, rather than pre-planned or formal responses: a mother tickling and verbalizing with her baby; a father playing peekaboo with his daughter with his serviette; a grandfather walking a toddler on his feet; sisters skipping together. Through positive and caring relationships, adults provide play spaces, time for playing, play resources and 'playful environments to enhance learning' (Luff, 2014b: 130).

Play is a fundamental part of children's quality of life, enshrined in the UNCRC (UN, 1989). Adults have the responsibility to provide for and support children's play entitlement. In nurseries in Reggio Emilia, the environment created and the opportunities provided are central to the ways in which play is allowed to develop and flourish by adults. Pedagogues working there value play as a right for all children to be protected and are committed to providing opportunities for children to play (Abbott and Nutbrown, 2001). The adults' commitment, vision, understanding and involvement in play recognizes that education is a product of a set of complex interactions, many of which can only be recognized when the environment is a fully participating element in education (Malaguzzi, 1996) and learning takes place in playful environments.

Developing playful learning involves understanding playful pedagogies. Playful learning communities involve playful adults as well as playful children, recognizing that adults have a key role in creating and sustaining playful learning environments, enabling participation and engagement for all children, with regard to diversity, children's heritage and the culture of the setting (Broadhead et al., 2010). Children learn to build on their knowledge and experience, and make connections through adult-led and child-initiated activities. When children are given appropriate opportunities, they use their culturally shaped funds of knowledge to create and sustain their play themes with other children, adults or parents (Broadhead et al., 2010). Play as an approach for learning is part of children's early education.

Play in early years education

The Plowden Report advocated the importance of play as a 'principle means of learning in early childhood' (CACE, 1967: 193) and the concept of 'learning through play' developed, as play helps children to make connections in their learning (Bruce, 2001). In thinking about young children's learning in early years education, Stephens (2006) identified an international theme showing the positive value of play. Recent research by play scholars investigating play (Moyles, 2010a) confirms that play is the most powerful medium for children's learning in the early years. While teachers and educationalists may advocate play practice, Howard (2014) highlights some barriers to play provision by teachers: a lack of confidence in using play in classroom activity; an intolerance of the mess created by some forms of play, like sand and water; increased class sizes, preventing the implementation of play-based curricula; the pressure to test and report on children's abilities; pressure from parents and carers towards the formal teaching of basic skills; and a lack of parental understanding about how play can enable children's learning.

The Schools Council project, Structuring Play (Manning and Sharp, 1977), integrated play and learning in early years education. Although the project is over 30 years old, the underlying principles of practice resonate with recent and current policy and play practice. The Foundation Stage curriculum (DfES, 2007) regarded well-planned play, both indoors and outdoors, as a key way in which children learn with enjoyment and challenge. The current EYFS curriculum (DfE, 2014a) promotes planned and purposeful play for children.

The Structuring Play project was based on the view that children in an infant school (aged 5–7 years) learn and develop through play; that play is a motivating factor for learning; and that adult help and participation are necessary for learning to take place. For play to promote learning, play must be structured for use as a teaching and learning medium. The teacher actively joins in children's play to further the learning experience and promote physical, cognitive, social and emotional development. In the Structuring Play project, through participation, initiation and intervention, teachers guided children's play through direct observation, responding to children's cues. Teachers provided first-hand, direct play experiences and contexts in which children could play and learn, establishing structured play areas for domestic play: a construction area, a make-believe area, an area for play with natural materials and an outdoor play area. In these contexts, children practise future roles, problem-solve, are creative, and develop language and mathematical reasoning.

Play-based learning is endorsed within early years policy in the UK. In early years provision in Scotland, play is central to how children learn, in developing both cognitive skills and softer skills around relating to other people. The Scottish government's Early Years Framework prioritizes play provision in developing play spaces and play opportunities for children and removing barriers to play (Scottish Government, 2008). Structured educational play activities are woven into learning experiences for children in the Foundation Phase curriculum for children in Wales. Play in active learning is an essential part of the children's curriculum (Welsh Government, 2008).

In a review of English policy documents (2000–2006), Moyles (2010a) identified that play can be adult-led as well as child-initiated, implying that play can be something other than child-led and free activity. A review of the EYFS curriculum in England by Tickell (2011), *The early years: foundations for life, health and learning*, identified that practitioners like the play-based approach of the EYFS curriculum, though with differing understandings of what learning through play actually means. Rogers (2000) highlights that understanding the pedagogy of play in the school context is complex and has a diversity of practice.

Tickell (2011) connects play with children's learning, as play helps young children develop the skills they need in order to become good learners. The EYFS curriculum (DfE, 2014a) views play as essential for children's development, building confidence as they learn to explore, to think about problems and to relate to others. Each area of learning and development is implemented through planned and purposeful play and through a mix of adult-led and child-initiated activity. Children learn by leading their own play and by taking part in play which is guided by adults.

In discussing ways adults support children's learning, Tickell (2011) recommends the use of play-based approaches combined with instructional yet 'playful teaching'. The Effective Provision of Pre-school Education (Sylva et al., 2004) study identified play as an element of effective educational pedagogy in the early years, involving interaction traditionally associated with teaching and also with the provision of instructive learning play environments and routines. In settings rated as excellent, provision included both teacher-initiated group work and child-initiated, freely chosen yet potentially instructive play activities (DfES, 2004a).

There are tensions in play pedagogy. Playful teaching as a concept justifies play to parents and others but has different intentions to child-led play and playful children (Moyles, 2010a). In the revised EYFS curriculum (DfE, 2014a), the notion of playful teaching is not included – practitioners are expected to provide a balance between activities led by children and activities led or guided by adults, responding to each child's emerging needs and interests, and guiding their development through warm, positive interaction. The EYFS (DfE, 2014a) document suggests that child-led playful learning is appropriate for young children – as they grow older, and as their development allows, it is expected that the balance will gradually shift towards more activities led by adults, to help children prepare for more formal learning, when they start full-time schooling at 5 years.

An emphasis on children's learning outcomes and on reporting of achievement in the EYFS and the Primary National Curriculum, can lessen the value of play as pedagogy for learning, as the quality of play is defined to the extent it improves children's outcomes and achievement, as measured at the end of the reception year by the EYFSP (Wood, 2010). Regarding play narrowly as defined educational outcomes within the current culture of product-led education, prevents practitioners and policy makers from understanding play as transformational agency for children (Wood, 2010) and that children, in their play, learn at their highest level (DfES, 2007). The purpose and value of playful learning will continue to be justified to some parents and carers who use their own experience of school as lesson-led activity as an expectation for their own child's schooling and experience of learning. The poem in the following story of practice is a way of sharing an understanding of play and playful learning with parents and carers.

Story of practice: What is play?

Ayna is a foundation stage teacher. During a welcome meeting for parents and carers of children starting the foundation stage unit, she reads the poem below . The poem prompted discussion about how children learn through play (Hallet, 2015).

The poem illustrates how children learn skills for life through playing. Playful learning concerns contexts for children to learn in a playful way.

Are the children *just playing* today?

You'll see lots of children playing today.
What are they doing with the bricks, dolls, paint and clay?
Why are they dressing up in clothes and with bags and hats?
What marks are they making on the paper with pencils and pens?
What are they finding out from the catalogue's print and pictures?
Who are they talking to, on the mobile phone?
What are they adding-up and taking-away in the shop?
Why are they riding bikes, cars and scooters in the yard outside?

Building with bricks helps them construct and build structures.
Playing with dolls helps them care and love.
Playing with paint and clay helps them imagine and create.
Playing with dressing-up clothes helps them understand who they are.
Playing with pens and paper helps them mark-make and write.
Playing with catalogues helps them engage with print and read.
Playing in a shop helps them add, subtract and calculate numbers.
Playing with a mobile phone helps them use technology and talk.
Playing with bikes, cars and scooters helps them understand space and direction.

So – are the children *just playing* today?
Through their play, the children are learning how to;
Care and love, build, create, imagine, write, read, talk and count.
Understand who they are and who they may become.
They are learning how to communicate and relate to others.
And to understand the everyday world they live in.
Yes, the children are just playing –
And – they are learning today, with their bricks, dolls, paint and clay.

Elaine Hallet

Implications for practice

By taking an inside-out perspective on children's play, a complex picture emerges of how children become successful players.

They see the world from the perspective of play, creating their own playful meanings, symbols and practices. They let play happen, by becoming immersed in the mood or spirit of play.

Wood's (2010 :18) view of play from the eyes of a child illustrates the importance of play for young children, which should be harnessed as a catalyst for learning in playful, authentic ways. For this to happen, those working with children should be able to articulate their pedagogy for playful learning to others, and provide playful environments, play resources and time for children to play in a sustained way, with sensitive interaction by adults as co-players and play facilitators.

 ## Further reading

Level 4

Moyles, J. (ed.) (2010) *Thinking about play: developing a reflective approach.* Maidenhead: Open University Press.
The chapters in this book cover a range of topics on play provision, including playful pedagogies and playful learning.

Level 5

Broadhead, P., Howard, J. and Wood, E. (eds) (2010) *Play and learning in the early years.* London: Sage.
This book examines theory, research, policy and practice around the relationship between play and learning, and play and pedagogy.

Level 6

Rogers, S. (ed.) (2011) *Rethinking play and pedagogy in early childhood education: concepts, contexts and cultures.* Abingdon: Routledge.
This book critically addresses contemporary international issues surrounding play and pedagogy.

NCTL Teachers' Standards (Early Years)

Standard 4.2
- Plan balanced and flexible activities and educational programmes that take into account the stage of development, circumstances and interests of children.

Bruce, T. (2011) *Learning through play: for babies, toddlers and young children.* London: Hodder & Stoughton.
Key ideas and best play practice for babies and young children are described and illustrated in this book.

Chapter 6

Early Language and Literacy

Chapter overview

This chapter examines the importance of children communicating through spoken and written symbols, exploring how children's early language and literacy develop. Two questions frame the discussion: (1) How do children get meaning from the *sounds* and *print* around them? (2) How do the *environment* and *adults* facilitate children's early language and literacy development?

Central to the discussion are: the notion of language and literacy as essential life skills; the relationship between language and thinking; the learning of language through social interaction; and children as symbol makers and users. Pedagogical approaches in early years education for language development and early reading and writing are discussed, including sustained shared thinking, the use of environmental print, playful reading and writing, and meaningful and purposeful literacy events. The role of parents and carers, practitioners, educators and teachers as demonstrators and influencers of literacy practices is explored. Stories of practice aid reflective thinking on providing for children's early language and literacy learning and development.

Language and literacy: skills for life

Babies are born into a world full of sound and pattern, decoding, encoding and evaluating meanings conveyed by printed symbols (Wray et al., 1989). Spoken language as the ability to communicate and literacy as the ability to read and write, are essential skills for life. The ability to engage in the environment and interact with the people who inhabit it, is key to living successfully in any culture. During my study visit to Japan, I travelled on the underground in Tokyo to schools to observe how literacy was taught; the notion of being literate in the environment that I temporarily lived in became very relevant as a non-literate person of Japanese, as I was surrounded by unfamiliar written symbols and spoken language (Hallet, 2008). The experience of navigating my way around the underground developed an awareness of a print-rich world, through the eyes of a young child, being surrounded by unfamiliar sounds, signs and symbols. I felt unsure and isolated in an unfamiliar environment. Each child's understanding of their world grows as they interact with adults, children and materials, and make meaning and sense of patterns, sounds and symbols. This social experience enables a child to live in a literate society (Wray et al., 1989), in which people are able to read and write, communicating through spoken language and written symbolic representation, such as marks, drawings, letters, words, numbers or music notation.

Language and thinking

In her seminal work *Children's minds*, Margaret Donaldson (1986) shows that language and thought are dependent on interpersonal contexts and how, given the support of such contexts, children can develop as thinkers and language users by the time they start school. Language helps cognitive development, as language is 'a tool of thought' (Bruner, cited in Whitebread, 2012: 126); with language, children make connections between the new and what is already known. Spoken language skills are also thinking skills; by listening to children talking, you know what they are thinking and how their language and minds are developing.

Sustained shared thinking (SST) as effective pedagogy for practice develops language and thinking. In SST, two or more individuals work together in an intellectual way to extend a narrative, evaluate activities, clarify a concept or solve a problem; both parties must contribute to the thinking and it must develop and extend in a sustained way (Siraj-Blatchford and Sylva, 2004). In episodes of SST, adults use open-ended questions to extend children's thinking and spoken language. Siraj et al. (2015) consider SST as a relational pedagogical strategy associated with child outcomes on the Sustained Shared Thinking and Emotional Well-being (SSTEW) scale for the provision of 2–5-year-olds. The SSTEW scale considers practice that supports children aged 2–5 years of age in developing skills in sustained shared thinking and emotional well-being, as well as developing strong relationships, effective communication and aspects of self-regulation.

In contextualized social interaction, children construct their own understandings through spoken language, then by internal language or thought within their minds. Vygotsky's social constructivist theory of learning included a further insight into language and thinking. Here, children can operate at a level of actual development on their own, but at a higher level when supported or scaffolded by an adult or a more experienced peer. This is described as their level of potential development (Whitebread, 2012) and is known as the zone of proximal development (ZPD). As pedagogical strategies for learning, SST and ZPD show the crucial role of the adult in supporting, scaffolding and extending children's thinking and language learning.

Learning language through social interaction

Pleasurable social interactions between adults and babies, such as smiling, pulling faces, blowing raspberries at one another, are frequently observed (Whitebread, 2012). Babies have a pre-disposition and an ability to interact with others, and adults to interact with babies, to read meaning into their actions and vocalizations. Adults modelling language and babies imitating through movement and vocalization is the beginning of language learning (Whitebread, 2012). Trevarthen and Aitken (2001) observed mother and child interactions to be important to establish children's ability to derive meaning from interaction. Calm and enjoyable interactions were dependent on sustained mutual attention and rhythmic synchrony of short 'utterances', which included vocalizations, touching, showing the face and hands, and gazing, all these expressions being performed with regulated reciprocity and turn taking.

Mutual attention between the adult and baby or young child is a key element in these joint-attention communicative episodes; this develops during the first two years of life (Whitebread, 2012). There are differences in the amount of time that 1- and 2-year-olds spend in joint-attention episodes with their parents and caregivers; this may be joint play, conversation, book reading. The variation affects the rate of a child's language development. There are also differences in the sensitivity or responsiveness of parents or caregivers in supporting children's language development. Adults who follow a child's attention, a child looking at or pointing at an object, use this as a basis for further interaction, including talk, while other adults switch the child's attention to their own point of focus, thus missing an opportunity to talk (Schaffer, 2004).

Babies and young children can spend a long part of their day out of their homes in daycare settings. Much of this time can be taken up with routines for an organized environment. In Goldschmied and Jackson's (2004) view, children require time with an adult to enable them to develop talk, so practitioners should be insightful and sit and relax with children, sharing something of their own interests. They suggest 'islands of intimacy' or 'island time', where a key person gives one child or a group of key children undivided attention as they wait for a nursery routine such as the setting up of lunch. Practitioners plan special times of day to capture babies and young children's interest when they share their personal collections of treasured objects: e.g. a set of shells, pebbles, marbles, ribbons, feathers, buttons, coins, lace bobbins, wooden carvings, fossils. The practitioner can convey their pleasure in handling the collection and tell stories about how the pieces were gathered, engaging children with the personal intimacy which this time offers. Children attending group settings spend much of their time in sharing time, space, toys and activities. 'Island time' (Nutbrown and Page, 2008) provides a unique few moments for children to spend with their key person and a distinctive collection as the context for a sensory language experience, as the following story of practice shows

Story of practice: island time

It was time for the practitioners to set the tables for mealtime, a time of change in routine that often became challenging for some children. Max, a key person, gathered three 18-month-old children onto cushions in the story corner of the setting. His special collection of pebbles was in the basket he was carrying; he explained he had collected them while walking his dog Millie on the beach. He tipped the pebbles onto the floor and the children reached for them, carefully picking them up, touching, smelling and handling them; they were variously smooth, rough, striped, small, large and of differing colours. Max acknowledged and reaffirmed their discoveries, extending their thinking and talk – 'mmm, the pebble has lots of colours: which do you like the best?' Max picked up the largest pebble, telling the children this was his dog Millie's favourite pebble as he threw it along the beach or into the sea for her to catch and bring back to him. Sometimes he threw it such a long way that Millie had to swim out into the sea to retrieve it; after bringing it back to him, she shook the water from her coat all over Max. The children imagined the scene and laughed at the image of their wet key person. After 10 minutes, the tables were set; the children helped to put the pebbles back into the basket and seemed disappointed to leave the pebbles and Millie the dog on the beach, but the smell of food indicated that their meal was ready.

Questions for reflection: island time

Considering any interests you have, can you make a special collection of objects you have gathered to share with the children? If so:

- What would your special collection be?
- What stories could you weave around the objects to capture children's imagination?
- How could you use your special collection of objects to help extend and develop children's language learning?

As a sensory language learning experience, island time demonstrates the central importance of context and meaningful interactions in adult–child relationships for the development of children's spoken language. The *Birth to three matters framework* (B-3) (Sure Start, 2002) recognizes the importance of young children being able to communicate. To become skilful communicators, babies and children need to be together with a key person and others in warm, loving and positive relationships, leading to the wider development of social relations, including friendship, a sharing of emotions and experiences and becoming a competent language user. Babies and children use their voices to make contact and to communicate their needs and feelings. In supporting children's early attempts at finding a voice, adults respond to their vocalizations by echoing, repeating and modelling language, reinforcing with praise, increasing confidence and encouraging children to both extend their talk and increase their communication skills. Babies and children learn to make sense of the sounds around them, respond differently to some sounds and are able to distinguish sound patterns; this auditory discrimination supports phonological awareness.

Babies and children from birth to 3 years of age start to learn about conversation, a reciprocal process of communication (Sure Start, 2002). This requires listening and responding, understanding the importance of paying attention to sounds and language, interpreting non-verbal signals, imitating, repeating and mirroring others. Children learn the rules of communication, such as turn taking, through making meaning with their key person, other supportive adults and older children. It is within these relationships and interactions that children's early attempts to converse are interpreted, responded to and valued.

Literacy learning

These language-learning experiences lay the foundation for early literacy learning. 'Communication and Language' is designated as a prime area of learning, with Literacy

(Reading and Writing) designated as a specific area of learning and development in the EYFS curriculum for children from birth to 5 years of age in England, reflecting the view that spoken language is the foundation for symbolic written representation.

The process of literacy learning and the ability to read and write are complex. The combination of visual and auditory awareness and recognition that print and written text have purpose and meaning, and that books are pleasurable, opening up new worlds, enables children's literacy learning (Merchant, 2008). Understanding how children learn to read and write has developed over the years from the concept of 'reading readiness', the theory that children are only taught to read at school, to 'emergent literacy', that is, children learn to read and write by interacting with the print around them, in the home and local community and in a print-rich environment in an early years setting and school. By being immersed in print, their literacy emerges (Gillen and Hall, 2003). This contrasts with the current emphasis on phonics in the teaching of reading – the skill of decoding sounds in words, particularly used in the programme of study of English in Primary National Curriculum, Key Stage 1 (DfE, 2014b) for children aged 5–7 years of age. Although the teaching of phonics is important, phonological decoding is only one strategy children use when reading, alongside using picture cues, context and word recognition.

Since the Rose Review (DfES, 2006), an independent review of the teaching of early reading, recommended the inclusion of a robust programme in the teaching of phonics, there has been a focus on this aspect of reading acquisition within the EYFS curriculum and the Primary National Curriculum in England. The Rose Review indicated that phonic work should be embedded within a broad, language-rich curriculum and in effective teaching, reading being taught in a multi-sensory way. Phonic skills for decoding words are essential for literacy, as are nurturing positive attitudes to language knowledge and skills and accessing them across the curriculum (DfES, 2006).

Clarke (1976), Goodman (1976) and Smith (1988) challenged the theory of 'reading readiness' developed by Partick (1899) and Huey (1908), that children are only ready to read when they begin school. Goodman proposed that children use meaning-making strategies for literacy, actively making sense of the world through engagement with literacy prior to starting school, as many children grow up in an urban environment that displays print everywhere. Ferriero and Teberosky (1982) argue that it is absurd to imagine that children do not develop any ideas about this cultural object until they find themselves in school and sitting in front of a teacher (all theorists cited in Hall et al., 2003).

In listing the type of print a young child is exposed to in their home and local environment, the range of multi-literacies on offer is vast and further expanded by technology; children engage in multi-modal literacy practices in the twenty-first-century digital age (Marsh, 2014). Print is found on cultural objects, in technology, on packaging and in advertising, as logos, words, numbers, on: toys, lunch boxes, sweet and crisp packets, shop names, clothing, shoes, bed linen, comics, magazines, books, leaflets, newspapers, catalogues, stickers, birthday cards, letters, notes, television, computer games, tablets, mobile phones, ipods, internet, music, billboards – the list is endless. Practitioners, educators, teachers and parents have a significant role to play in helping children to engage in the patterns of print and pictorial images around them and to gain meaning from them, as demonstrated in this story of practice.

Story of practice: reading patterns

Isla is an early years teacher. Inspired by attending a course on using environmental print with children, she took a group of 4-year-olds to the school car park to look at number plates on the cars. Standing in a safe place, she asked the children if they could recognize a number and read it out loud. Their non-response puzzled her and she realized that the black pattern of letters and numbers was just that to the young children – undistinguishable shapes and marks. She began pointing to the letters and numbers, naming them and connecting them to the children: 'Look, that's a number 4. How old are you, Amy? [4] Well, that number says how old you are'; 'Can anyone see the first letter of their name? Yes, that letter "M" is at the beginning of your name, "Molly"'. Isla was helping the children decode and make sense of the patterns before them.

This story of practice shows the essential role of adults in helping children to interact with print and gain meaning from it. Children first encounter literacy practices and resources in the home, where parents, carers, older siblings and extended family members demonstrate purposeful reading and writing practices: reading a newspaper, magazine or book for pleasure, reading information on the internet, writing a birthday card and addressing the envelope, reading a take-away food menu for their phone order, writing appointments and events on the calendar in the kitchen. The home-based practice of an adult reading a bedtime story to their child, prompting an enjoyment of books, can lead to children becoming avid readers, and reading for pleasure has a long-term influence on vocabulary. Research by Sullivan and Brown (2014) shows the connection between reading for pleasure and intellectual development up to the age of 16. Children who read avidly at 10 years of age had better vocabularies by the time they got to age 42 than children who did not. Developing good reading habits in childhood has lifelong benefits, with children continuing as readers into adulthood.

Adults who share literacy practices and events with children enable them to join a literacy club of people using literacy in meaningful ways (Smith,1971; Hall, 1987); once part of this club children have access to the literate society and culture in which they live. Literacy as a social practice (Smith, 1971) cannot be divorced from language as a whole, nor from its wider cultural context. Literacy is given meaning by the cultural discourses in which it is embedded; young children from birth are witnesses to and participants in literacy practices. Children learn the rules of literacy and understand the meaning of print through engagement with the print-rich environment around them (Gillen and Hall, 2003). How do children represent this meaning?

Children as symbol makers and users

For children to develop as readers and writers, they need to become symbol makers and symbol users. Being able to represent experiences by making images or symbols that stand for people, events and objects, in their absence or in their presence, is an important part of becoming literate (Bruce and Spratt, 2008). The concept from Reggio Emilia nurseries, that of a child having a 'hundred voices' with which to communicate (Malaguzzi, 1996), resonates with the notion of 'multimodal literacies' (Flewitt, 2008) in terms of how meaning is expressed through different modes of representation – not just words, but combinations of different modes, such as words, images, sounds and movement. Different modes are used in different kinds of literacy practices: spoken language and sound effects are often used in conversation, singing songs, telling and reading stories aloud, playing digital games; written language symbols are used in music notation, handwriting and printed texts such as comics and magazines; visual images are used to create drawings, three-dimensional models on television, video and computer games (Makin and Jones Diaz, 2004). Most forms of literacy combine modes, and children in the early years of education can be encouraged to develop critical literacy (Flewitt, 2008), to select the most effective modes to convey their message.

In their symbolic representation, children exploring written symbols don't differentiate between drawing, letters and numbers in their mark making, as shown in Figure 6.1 (Hallet, 1990: 7). Here, a 4-year-old represents herself playing with her friend, the happy mood represented by the symbol of sunshine and a rainbow. She surrounds herself playing with written letters and marks. These are significant marks: E and P, representing herself (Ella) and her friend Poppy, frequently appear.

This child's drawing shows the relationship between children and written language, termed by Gillen and Hall (2003: 9) as 'early childhood literacy', a concept that allows children to use modes of literacy, as appropriate and meaningful to them. Early childhood literacy is not about emergence or becoming literate but about children *being* literate. Early childhood literacy allows literacy practices and products to be acknowledged as valid in their own right, rather than

Figure 6.1 Symbolic representations

perceived as incorrect examples of adult literacy. This concept allows early literacy to move away from the constraints of the classroom and to extend to interaction between people and places (Gillen and Hall, 2003) – a social construct of early literacy learning that is evolving through the developing digital age of social media and children's use of technology. In examining the use of touch-screen tablets in Australian pre-schoolers, Neumann (2014) found that many children interact with touch-screens at home. Children with greater access to touch-screen tablets were found to have higher letter-sound and name-writing skills. Tablets have the potential to foster emergent literacy, although this may depend on the quality of the digital interactions.

Real-life literacy

There is a division between the way literacy is treated in education within the school context, as decontextualized literacy tasks, and the way literacy is used in the every-day world which young children inhabit (Gillen and Hall, 2003). Children need space and time to explore the use of literacy as something meaningful and purposeful in people's lives. Real-life literacy experiences are always meaningful to people, as literacy is related to their lives, interests and concerns (Hall, 1999). In everyday life, literacy makes things happen: following instructions on the car's satnav to reach the right destination, reading labels on food packages to ensure we eat the right food, writing letters to make sure our views are known. Literacy can be imposed on children as exercises, so they become responders rather than initiators.

Socio-dramatic play has a powerful role in providing opportunities for children to be literacy users and makers, rather than analysers of literacy (Hall, 1999), giving children choices and contexts for meaningful literate behaviours. Socio-dramatic play gives children the opportunity for playful reading and writing (Brock and Ranklin, 2008). Although teachers may designate a play area as a hospital, garage, home, space rocket or three bears' cottage, and provide appropriate materials and resources, once inside the play area children are able to make choices, and the way the play progresses is usually determined by children and always meaningful to children, as within play, literacy acts occur within meaningful situations.

Teachers and educators can extend children's knowledge of literacy within play by developing literacy practices alongside children's choices, not instead of them. Hall (1999) highlights that creating events, happenings and problems meaningful to the theme of play can encourage further literacy engagement. Hall describes one such event in a play area: a notice appeared on the sweet shop door from the council, saying it had to close due to a new road being built. This prompted the children to write letters and make leaflets, signs and billboards for their protest march to keep the sweet shop open. Similarly, an event within a child's neighbourhood can prompt a meaningful context for purposeful writing, as the following story of practice shows.

Story of practice: Gabrielle's letter

Gabrielle, who is 3 years old, is walking home from her nursery with her grandma; she likes to skip along ahead, but along the way there are roadworks as the street lights are being replaced, resulting in an uneven surface along the pavement which makes her fall over and scrape her knees. At home, as Grandma puts plasters on her knees, Gabrielle says, 'it wasn't my fault I fell down, it was the pavement's fault', asking her grandma why the pavement was rough. Grandma explains: 'The road men have dug some holes in the pavement to put some new street lights in, to make the road brighter for car drivers to see down the road.' Gabrielle considers this: 'But it makes the pavement dangerous. I'm going to write a letter to the road men telling them about my fall.' Gabrielle had seen her mother and grandma write letters and Grandma helps Gabrielle write her letter.

(Continued)

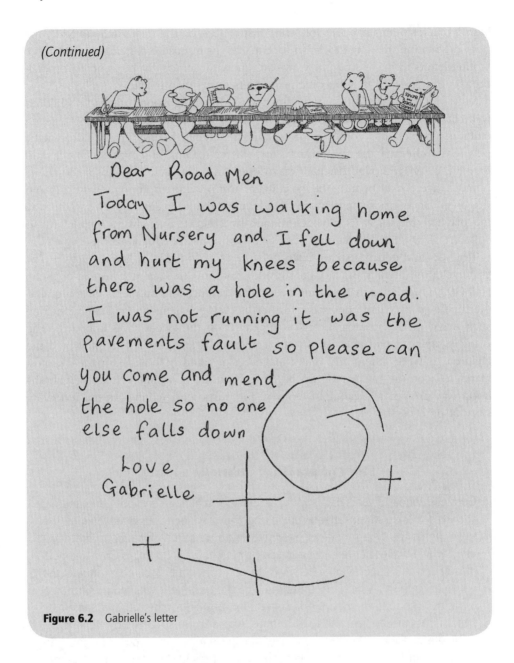

(Continued)

Dear Road Men

Today I was walking home from Nursery and I fell down and hurt my knees because there was a hole in the road. I was not running it was the pavements fault so please can you come and mend the hole so no one else falls down

Love
Gabrielle

Figure 6.2   Gabrielle's letter

This story of practice shows that families are important influences on children's early literacy practices. As demonstrators of literacy practice, Gabrielle had seen her mother and grandma write letters and followed their example in writing for a purpose.

The ORIM framework (Nutbrown et al., 2005) promotes four literacy practices for parents and family members to help in a child's literacy development:

Opportunities for literacy

Parents and family members provide opportunities for children's literacy development, such as giving children books or writing materials, and singing nursery rhymes, listening to and playing musical sounds with them.

Recognition of children's literacy

Parents and family members provide encouragement by recognizing and valuing children's early achievements in reading, mark making, writing, identifying letters and logos.

Interaction around literacy

Children need their parents and family members to interact with them, sharing with them and supporting them in real-life literacy tasks where children can make a meaningful contribution, such as writing a birthday card.

Models of literacy users

Parents and family members can act as influential models of users of literacy if children see them using literacy themselves in everyday life, such as reading a newspaper, writing notes or following written instructions.

The ORIM framework provides a structure for parents and families in supporting children's early literacy development. Similarly, the framework can be used to consider how teachers provide literacy practices for children's early literacy development by providing opportunities and meaningful playful contexts for literacy, using environmental print, books, early writing and spoken language, and positive interactions with adults who demonstrate, model, influence and recognize children's literacy development and achievements.

Implications for practice

Children must have access to a literate environment.
Children must have access to literate adults.
Children must have opportunities to practise literacy.

(Continued)

(Continued)

These are the three conditions necessary for the creation of a curriculum which supports children's literacy knowledge, skills and understanding (Hall, 1987: 16). They demonstrate essential holistic and contextualized conditions for children to become confident language and literacy users and makers. The current climate of government policy in England and developing preferred literacy practices, like teaching synthetic phonics in a decontextualized way, could counteract meaningful literacy pedagogy and practice.

The notion of language and literacy as life skills is central to language and literacy practices that enable children's talking, reading and writing in meaningful contexts. The role of parents and families, educators and teachers, as demonstrators and facilitators of language and literacy, providing opportunities for literacy engagement and interaction, recognizing and valuing children's language and literacy ability, and encouraging meaningful, purposeful and real-life language and literacy experiences, is essential for early language and literacy learning and development. These experiences give children language and literacy knowledge, understanding and skills for life.

 ## Further reading

Level 4

Neaum, S. (2012) *Language and literacy for the early years*. London: Sage.
With practical guidance on how to support children's language acquisition, language acquisition and development are the focus of this book.

Level 5

Marsh, J. and Hallet, E. (eds) (2008) *Desirable literacies: approaches to language and literacy in the early years* (2nd edn). London: Sage.
This book demonstrates the importance of providing meaningful, purposeful opportunities for children to develop as literacy learners, offering a range of practical ideas for how this can be achieved.

Chapter 3 of this book ('Signs and symbols: children's engagement with environmental print' by Hallet) provides a comprehensive discussion on children's engagement with environmental print in home and classroom contexts, and offers a wide range of literacy practices for use with children.

Level 6

Gillen, J. and Hall, N. (2001) '"Hiya, Mum!" An analysis of pretence telephone play in a nursery setting', *Early Years*, 1: 15–24.

This journal article discusses research on children's spoken language through telephone talk in a themed pretence play setting.

NCTL Teachers' Standards (Early Years)

Standard 2.4

- Lead and model effective strategies to develop and extend children's learning and thinking, including sustained shared thinking.

Siraj, I., Kingston, D. and Melhuish, E. (2015) *Assessing quality in early childhood education and care: sustained shared thinking and emotional well-being (SSTEW) scale for 2–5-year-olds provision*. London: IOE Press.

The SSTEW scale considers high-quality pedagogy and practice for young children, particularly sustained shared thinking and children's well-being.

Standard 3.4

- Demonstrate a clear understanding of synthetic phonics in the teaching of early reading.

Glazzard, J. and Stokoe, J. (2013) *Teaching systematic phonics and early English*. Northwich: Critical Publishing.

This book concerns the teaching of English in the primary years, placing systematic synthetic phonics within the context of early English.

Chapter 7

Creative Children

Chapter overview

This chapter explores the development of children's creativity in the broadest sense; defining creativity, discussing children's creative thinking, symbolic representation and thinking in drawing and schematic play, creativity in education and curriculum, and creative learning and the role of practitioners, educators and teachers in providing opportunities for children's creativity. Pedagogical approaches to creativity, including possibility thinking, sustained shared thinking, play and creative pedagogy for learning, are considered. There is an opportunity to reflect on children's creativity and to consider creative practice.

Creativity

Young children being creative in the early years is often associated with art-based activities, like painting, colouring, sticking, drawing, taking place on the 'creative table' in an early years setting or classroom, or on the kitchen table in a home-based context; however, it is much more than this. Creativity involves the ability to see things in fresh ways, learning from past experiences and relating this learning to new experiences. Duffy (2006) defines creativity as the ability to think along unorthodox lines and to break barriers, using non-traditional approaches to solve problems, going further than the information given and creating something unique or original. Creativity is more than the arts; it is a way of thinking and doing and being creative. Creativity, a key cross-curricular thinking skill, has huge implications for future society (Craft, 2002). Innovations in science and medicine, such as space travel and the invention of penicillin, have impacted on the development of society. Creative thinking enables people to challenge, to think beyond existing traditions, to adapt to a changing society, to be original and unique (Craft, 2002). Creative thinkers invent, create, play, imagine, theorize, experiment, are resourceful and take risks. Creative people are found in the arts and sciences as artists, actors, dancers, musicians, writers, poets, scientists and mathematicians.

Creativity in education

Practitioners, educators and teachers should encourage creativity to promote the highest levels of thinking, originality, innovation, resourcefulness, individuality, vision, initiative and self-expression, as well as artistry (Craft, 2002). Educational policy can help or hinder the development of creative children. Progressive education policy in the 1960s and 1970s promoted creativity through the teaching of music, drama, the creative arts and performance arts. Government policy in the 1980s and 1990s focused on the teaching of the 'three Rs' (reading, writing and arithmetic), with the view that children needed a basic education to be literate and numerate, without a focus on fostering creativity and independence of thought (Fumoto et al., 2012). In the 2000s, creativity is included in the UK's national education agenda. The National Advisory Committee on Creative and Cultural Education's (NACCCE) report, *All our futures: creativity, culture and education* (1999) emphasized the importance of creative and cultural development through education to promote the personal, intellectual, social and economic development of children and young people. The report influenced current educational policy and practice (Fumoto et al., 2012) in the early years and primary curricula.

Creativity is included in the early years curricula in the four countries of the UK, described as: Creative Development (Wales), Expressive Arts (Scotland), The Arts

(Northern Ireland), Expressive Arts and Design (England). In the Foundation Stage in Northern Ireland (CCEA, 2014: 1), 'The Arts' is defined as follows:

> Children's creative, expressive and physical development is closely linked with all aspects of their learning. Children should be given opportunities to explore and share their thoughts, ideas and feelings through a variety of art and design, music, movement, dance, dramatic and role-play activities. Through taking part in a range of well-planned activities, children's fine and gross motor skills will develop, they will gain confidence in what they can do and this will help build their self-esteem.

The Early Years Foundation Stage curriculum in England (DfE, 2014a: 8) defines this Area of Learning 'Expressive Arts and Design' as:

> Expressive arts and design involves enabling children to explore and play with a wide range of media and materials, as well as providing opportunity and encouragement for sharing their thoughts, ideas and feelings through a variety of activities in art, movement, dance, role-play, design and technology.

In these two definitions, an emphasis on creativity as an arts-based activity prevails, as creativity is demonstrated in young children's art-making processes. Art, particularly drawing, enables children to make meaning and represent the world around them.

Children's drawings

Children's drawings 'open a window into their realities and how they shape these' (Wright, 2010: 11). The constructive process of drawing helps children shape, order and understand their experience; drawing activity defines their reality. Through drawing and talking, children come to know reality by creating it. For practitioners, educators and teachers, it is essential to understand what is meant by a child's drawing in relation to her/his ideas, actions and feelings. How adults interpret a child's symbolic representation in their drawing can influence how a child may continue or extend their drawing (Wright, 2010). Observing what a child actually does while drawing helps children's creative involvement in the art-making process (Potter and Edens, 2001). Adults need to go with the flow of children's thinking and symbolic representation, requiring sensitive participation with children while they are drawing. These joint involvement episodes require empathy with the child's artistic experience and the materials they are working with (Kolbe, 2000). By being with the child, adults can often sustain or extend the child's interest and involvement. Looking at the relationships between graphic, narrative and embodied components of the artwork, a child's ideas and feelings will unfold, and adults are able to understand the artwork's purpose and function. Seeing beyond the marks and forms children make, appreciating children's visual thinking (Kolbe, 2000), provides opportunity for educators and teachers to extend children's thinking and learning with appropriate resources and intervention. A schema demonstrates children's thinking, described by Atherton and Nutbrown (2013: 9) as 'a mental representation that mediates activity' and that can be represented in children's drawings.

Schema and creativity

The work of Chris Athey in the1980s and 1990s aided the understanding of schemas in early years practice (Atherton and Nutbrown, 2013). Schemas are patterns of thinking and behaviours of organizing knowledge and experience (Beals, 1998). Children can demonstrate schema through play activity. A child displaying Vertical Schema may continually play with toys that go up and down; they may want their teddy to go up in a rocket to the moon and land back down; they might make their cars, aeroplanes, helicopters fly up in the air; they may repeatedly drop their toys from their high chair or buggy (Constable, 2013). Children display Enclosure Schema by being interested in edges and ends of things and find ways to make separate and enclosed spaces; they would want a fence or structure to go right round them or a field for their pony to go in, rather than just a track for it to walk on. Children in Enveloping Schema enjoy the feeling of being secure, wrapped in something or hiding under blankets. They may make dens, by moving furniture to hide behind or moving a blanket from their bed to hide under. They may also wrap their toys, post things in the swing bin or hide objects in drawers or cupboards (Constable, 2013). Enclosure and Enveloping Schema overlap; through observation, schema dominance can be identified. Therefore, practitioners, educators and teachers require an understanding of schema to extend children's thinking with appropriate resources – for example, baskets, small boxes, small-world toys, handkerchiefs, in the Enveloping Schema, with adults using vocabulary such as 'in', 'putting', 'covering' to extend the language in the play activity.

Figure 7.1 is a 3-year-old's drawing, demonstrating how reading beyond a young child's visual representation illuminates her enclosure schema, thinking and early writing development. The large circle encloses smaller circular marks and dots; a further circle marked with lines is positioned outside the enclosure. Beyond the schema representation, early letter formation appears in her mark making as circular shapes and lines found in alphabetic letter shapes – for example, a, o, i, l, t.

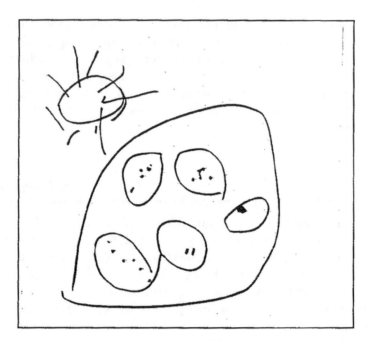

Figure 7.1   Enclosure schema

Creative thinking

The notion that creative people are located solely in the arts is challenged by Siraj-Blatchford (2007), as creativity is a universal capability; everyone has creative potential (Runco, 2003) and the ability to think creatively. Creative thinking concerns thinking that is novel, producing ideas that are of value (Sternberg, 2003) or something that is new for the individual. The extent to which something is viewed as creative involves a value judgement (NACCCE, 1999); others – these could be children as well as adults in early years contexts – must agree it is creative. Creative thinking highlights the connections between critical thinking and problem solving (Fumoto et al., 2012), as creativity is about both problem setting and problem solving, with meaningful solutions being formed (Wright, 2010). The notion of evaluative thinking (NACCCE, 1999) suggests that creative thinking always includes some critical thinking; both are interdependent (Lipman, 2003).

Talking and social interaction are key elements within creative thinking, highlighting the importance of adults modelling, questioning and making their own thinking explicit to children in contexts in which children articulate their thinking and enjoy playing around with ideas (Whitebread, 2000). Sustained shared thinking develops creative and critical thinking through collaborative talk. Two or more adults and children work together to solve a problem, clarify a concept, evaluate an activity, extend a narrative, in a sustained way. Young children's problem solving improves in collaboration, with partners scaffolding understanding (Siraj-Blatchford, 2007). Smith et al. (2003: 35) found children working in friendship pairs to be more successful in problem-solving activities than non-friends. Children in novice–expert pairs can show significant improvement in their problem-solving tasks (Katz and Chard, 2000).

The creation of an atmosphere in which *talking about* thinking happens and children are encouraged to *reflect on* their thinking (Trickey and Topping, 2004), is important. Pedagogic strategies, such as sustained shared thinking and possibility thinking, as 'cognitive apprenticeship' approaches (McGuinness, 1999), use scaffolding techniques as successful interventions when they frame young children's learning in meaningful contexts (Donaldson, 1986). The emphasis on known and meaningful contexts underpins young children's creative activity, as they use recalled experiences to imagine something new and to innovate (Vygotsky, 2004).

Creative learning

The concept of 'possibility thinking' (Craft, 2002), to aid children's ability to formulate 'what if' questions in collaboration with others, supports the notion of 'creative learning' (Craft et al., 2008), in which creativity and creative thinking become part of children's education, developing creative and imaginative children. Creativity should be a usual cross-curricular approach to learning rather than a bolt-on activity (Duffy, 2006). The construct of creativity in the teaching of children is defined in six strands by Beetlestone (1998): (1) creativity is a form of learning, which concerns (2) representation, (3) originality, (4) thinking creatively, (5) problem solving, and (6) mood/drive as a source of creativity.

Creativity is defined by Duffy (2006) as a process for learning with two elements – creativity as it relates to children's mastery over equipment and materials, such as teaching a young child how to hold a paintbrush correctly and how to mix paint, and the creative process as it relates to exploring ideas. Duffy's (2006) model of the creative process in young children provides a framework for supporting children's creativity and imagination in the early years:

- **Curiosity**
  - What is it?
- **Exploration**
  - What can or does it do?

- **Play**

    o What can I do with it?

- **Creativity**

    o What can I create or invent?

The creative process involves an emotional interaction between the individual and their environment (Craft, 2002); the person, the product, the process and the environment form creativity (Fumoto et al., 2012). An understanding of convergent and divergent thinking aids children's creative development. Convergent thinkers have the ability to find one correct answer to a problem, which involves logical deductive reasoning – the next number in the sequence '2, 4, –' is? Divergent thinking concerns the development of many different solutions to an open-ended problem: how many uses can you think of for an orange? (Fumoto et al., 2012). Divergent thinkers make imaginative connections. The common use of templates, colouring sheets and worksheets in early years practice promotes convergent thinkers, rather than divergent thinkers with imagination and originality.

How do educators and teachers provide a creative learning environment? The following story of practice shows an open-ended, playful learning environment that enabled the children to think creatively, problem-solve and make original products in a creative way.

Story of practice: Highfield Design Centre

The topic 'Materials' led to the establishing of a design centre in a classroom for 8-year-olds to engage in creative playful thinking and learning. Literacy resources, construction toys, junk materials and art resources were provided in the area, the children were left alone and the Highfield Design Centre started to come to life through role-play involving talking, listening, reading, writing, drawing and making. The notebook on the table at reception was soon becoming full of customers' enquiries and orders, and their contact details; completed orders were recorded in the book. Lists were put up around the design centre and used as work schedules – see Figure 7.2.

The children were beginning to organize the activity in the design centre. An argument was overheard: 'I want to be boss.' ... 'Well, I want to be boss.' ... 'No you're not, I am!' The children were beginning to solve the problem of who was in charge of activity in the design centre. The teacher decided to sensitively intervene by building on children's conversation and thinking:

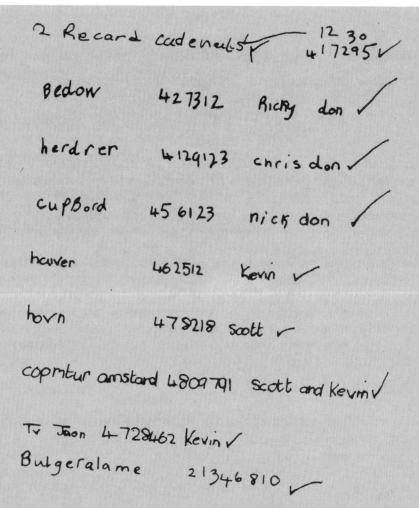

Figure 7.2 Customers' orders

'Who do you think would work in a design centre? What jobs need to be done?' A list of people to work in Highfield Design Centre was compiled: a designer, a manager, a secretary, a manufacturer, the boss, a quality controller and a stores person. A discussion took place about jobs in the design centre and what role in the design and production process the children would take. The children wrote job descriptions for each job role, identifying what skills and qualities were required for each job. For example:

(Continued)

(Continued)

The Secretary

To do this job you will have to listen on the telephone what needs to be designed for the people who ring up. You will also have to sort out what time it is convenient for a meeting with the boss or manager. You will also need to write on the computer.

Who would do which job? The problem was solved by an application process. After reading the job description, each child completed an application form and was interviewed by a panel of children for suitability for each job. Once successful, name badges such as 'I am the boss' were made and worn. The design centre was now clearly organized; the children had defined roles and responsibilities, and the centre was ready for production.

Designing and making products

Dear Highfield Design Centre,

I have had an important call that 14 plates are needed next week. Please could you get them by tomorrow and also somebody in Toronto needs 400 tea cups by Friday.

From Your Boss

Orders for products were received. One order had a design brief with an open-ended request 'to make something useful'. The class was divided into design teams of two children in a team. The pairs worked creatively together on their design plans, annotating the designs with notes about suitable materials and construction notes on how the design would be made. The design teams then made their design with the construction toys, junk materials and art resources available, producing original products. The centre's shelves became full of original and uniquely designed items like money boxes, a machine that cooks you dinner, a machine that cleans things up, a mobile oven, a day-and-night pencil holder and a remote control television.

The design centre became full of products; they had to be sold to release more shelf space. How could this problem be solved? Through discussion, the children realized that before buying something, it is usual to read information about it. Each design team wrote a leaflet giving details about their product, trying to persuade people to buy it; the leaflets were put in the design centre. The teams went with their product to 'sell it' to children in other classes with a short presentation. The children listened, asked questions and critically judged the usefulness of the products.

The design centre provided a meaningful context for children to engage in a creative way, solving problems through creative thinking, being creative by using open-ended materials to create something original.

Questions for reflection: creativity

These questions will help you consider the provision of creativity in your setting or school as a practitioner, educator or teacher, or as a student on a work placement (adapted from Duffy, 2006: 145):

- How does the *indoor* provision in your setting or school promote creativity? Are there limitations? How can any limitations be overcome?
- How does the *outdoor* provision in your setting or school promote creativity? Are there any limitations? How can any limitations be overcome?
- How are children organized to promote *opportunities* for creativity? How can opportunities be further created?
- How are *resources* used? Can they be used more effectively?
- How are available *adults* used? Can they be used more effectively?

Children with one hundred languages

The construct of a young child in Reggio Emilia, as a creative child with a hundred languages to communicate and express themselves, and a being with extraordinary potential, contrasts with the emerging construct of children in England – an empty vessel into which the right ingredients of knowledge and skills must be poured (Jones, 2012). In their approach to creative learning, pedagogues working in Reggio Emilia nurseries place great emphasis on encouraging curiosity, with both children and pedagogues engaged in a constant process of discovery. The child is not seen as a passive recipient of education or care, but as an active, creative participant (Jones, 2012). The environment is regarded as a teacher, a motivating and cognitive force in creating spaces for relationships, options, emotionality, thinking and creativity (Malaguzzi, 1996: 3). Children participate in projects often instigated by a provocation, such as a zebra appearing at a window: How did it get there? What is it doing? Has it escaped from a zoo? How will we get it back there? (Sightlines, 1996). The children are able to work on projects over extended periods of time – a term or a year – going back to their drawing, sculpture or dance, drafting and redrafting their thinking and work. This is in contrast to the approach in some settings and schools in the UK, where young children's completed clay models are squashed up and returned to the clay bucket. The opportunity to go back and add to their model, as a sculptor would, is denied; the emphasis is on the end product of creativity, rather than on the process of creative learning, as in Reggio Emilia settings. The poem, 'No Way. The Hundred is There' (Loris Malaguzzi, 1996: 3; translated by Lalla Gandini), describes the image of the creative child in Reggio Emilia pedagogy who influences pedagogy, provision and practice.

No Way. The Hundred is There

The child
is made of one hundred.
The child has
a hundred languages
a hundred hands
a hundred thoughts
a hundred ways of thinking
of playing, of speaking.
A hundred, always a hundred
ways of listening
of marvelling, of loving
a hundred joys
for singing and understanding
a hundred worlds
to discover
a hundred worlds
to invent
a hundred worlds
to dream.
The child has
a hundred languages
(and a hundred, hundred, hundred more)
but they steal ninety-nine.
The school and the culture
separate the head from the body.
They tell the child:
to think without hands
to do without head
to listen and not to speak
to understand without joy
to love and marvel
only at Easter and Christmas.

They tell the child:
to discover the world already there
and of the hundred
they steal ninety-nine.
They tell the child:
that work and play
reality and fantasy
science and imagination
sky and earth
reason and dream
are things
That do not belong together.

And thus they tell the child
that the hundred is not there.
The child says:
No way. The hundred is there.

Implications for practice

Creativity recognizes young children's potential and their originality.

In facilitating young children's potential for creative thinking and originality, this concept of creativity (Fumoto et al., 2012: 28) echoes Malaguzzi's (1996) poem, 'No Way. The Hundred is There', demonstrating the importance of pedagogy for creativity, how an open-ended approach can facilitate the development of creative children and how a closed approach can hinder creativity. It is important for practitioners, educators and teachers to use an open-ended creative pedagogy to learning and teaching for children to become creative. To understand the importance of creativity in children's learning is to provide opportunities to open up children's potential as learners, creators, discoverers, inventors, experimenters, risk-takers and problem-solvers.

 Further reading

Level 4

Duffy, B. (2006) *Supporting creativity and imagination in the early years* (2nd edn). Maidenhead: Open University Press.

There are examples of good practice and practical guidance in this book to help children learn through the arts.

Level 5

Wright, S. (2012) *Understanding creativity in early childhood*. London: Sage.
This book examines how children make meaning through drawings and narrative play.

Level 6

Siraj-Blatchford, I. (2007) 'Creativity, communication and collaboration: the identification of pedagogic progression in sustained shared thinking', *Asia-Pacific Journal of Research in Early Childhood Education*, 1 (2) 3–23.
This journal article develops thinking about creativity as pedagogic practice.

NCTL Teachers' Standards (Early Years)

Standard 3.3
- Demonstrate a critical understanding of the EYFS areas of learning and development and engage with the educational continuum of expectations, curricula and teaching of Key Stages 1 and 2.

Duffy, B. (2010) 'Creativity across the curriculum', in C. Cable, L. Miller and G. Goodliff (eds) *Working with children in the early years* (2nd edn). Abingdon: Routledge.
Chapter 13 in this book discusses creativity as part of every area of the curriculum, providing creative and imaginative learning experiences for children.

Chapter 8

Children Exploring

Chapter overview

Children's exploratory and investigative learning for developing knowledge and understanding about the world in which they live is the focus of this chapter. The role of practitioners, educators and teachers in creating enabling environments for children to explore, investigate and discover is discussed. Provision for children to problem-solve, investigate and inquire for mathematical and scientific knowledge, understanding and development of skills is considered through examples of pedagogy and practice in enabling children's exploratory learning within outdoor and indoor spaces. The teachers' and educators' role in facilitating exploratory, investigative and inquiry learning is considered, with opportunity to reflect on examples of practice.

An enabling environment

Babies are born into an unknown world of people and places; they are born curious and try out new things through exploring the world in which they find themselves. Practitioners, educators and teachers are responsible for providing an appropriate, safe learning environment where children can develop curiosity and resilience. Dukes and Smith (2014) highlight that the absence of such an enabling environment can encourage children to become passive and indifferent, rather than exploratory, curious, investigative and questioning children who learn by playing, exploring, actively learning, creating and thinking critically.

A principle of practice in the EYFS curriculum in England that should shape practice in early years settings, identifies that 'children learn and develop well in enabling environments, in which their experiences respond to their individual needs' (DfE, 2014a: 6). Johnston (2012) defines an enabling environment as one in which children interact with others (adults and other children) in a rich stimulating learning environment that encourages children to explore the world around them, learn to relate to others and become well-rounded individuals, who are socially and emotionally able to interact in the wider world. An enabling environment encourages children's individuality and independence. Moyles (2010) argues that a flexible pedagogy to provision and practice, encouraging discovery, exploratory and child-centred play, is more effective in developing inquiring children than didactic, controlling approaches that adversely affect behaviour and motivation for learning.

'Understanding the world' as an area of learning in the EYFS curriculum involves guiding young children to make sense of their physical world and their community through opportunities to explore, observe and find out about people, places, technology and the environment (DfE, 2014a). Selbie and Wickett (2010) view the adult's role as one that provides enabling indoor and outdoor contexts through positive nurturing relationships to help babies and young children travel their unique learning journey of exploration and discovery.

The introduction of the EYFS curriculum in England (DCSF, 2008) promoted the importance of both indoor and outdoor environments as spaces for learning for children under 5 years of age The notion of continuous provision connecting learning in indoor and outdoor contexts, integrates learning in a holistic way. In both indoor and outdoor provision, the setting, school or childminder's home should be an environment that encourages children to be independent and curious, following their own individual avenues for exploration (Johnston, 2012). Closed resources like pre-drawn worksheets for colouring activity predict children's play and restrict children's independence in learning (Dukes and Smith, 2014). Open-ended resources, such as cardboard boxes, blocks, duplo, collections of objects such as shells or pebbles, natural materials such as stones, sticks, sand and water, playdough and magnifying glasses, encourage children's exploratory play and investigation.

Outdoor play resources found in many nurseries and reception classes, like bikes, pedal cars, balls, beanbags and play equipment, such as climbing frames, encourage the development of gross motor skills through physical play (Johnston, 2012). There needs to be sufficient space outdoors for energetic play (DCSF, 2008), and also quiet areas where children can sit on a wooden chair, stool or bench with chalk boards to write on or books to read, enjoy contemplation and reflection, find a tent or den to hide in, an umbrella, parasol or weeping willow tree to be sheltered by. All these resources provide contemplative and reflective spaces for children to spend time in.

Young children are naturally curious and use their senses to touch, taste, smell and listen to things as they encounter the world around them. An outdoor space should provide opportunities for sensual experience to encourage children to use all their senses (Johnston, 2005). A sensory garden area provides changing colour in leaves and flowers through the seasons; smells through herbs and flowers; tastes through the vegetables and fruit grown there; different textures to touch, like stones, moss, bark and leaves (Johnston, 2012). Children explore the living world by using magnifying glasses to see insects and butterflies more closely, and binoculars to observe birds flying and feeding from feeders in trees. In the following story of practice, Salma, an early years educator, explains how she developed an enabling outdoor environment for children in her community nursery.

Story of practice: creating an outdoor space

Our community nursery is part of a newly built children's centre, and the outdoor space was a tarmacked area surrounded by grassy banks. A covered area from the indoor space to the outdoor space provided a transitional area for children to paint, chalk or play in the sandpit and water tray. I wanted to establish an outdoor space with different areas for children to explore. I had a limited budget so decided to make the areas from local recycled materials. I got used tyres from the garage down the road; these became planting containers for growing herbs and lavender. Old railway sleepers were made into raised beds to grow vegetables, salad and flowers. A pile of wood became a home for insects for the children to investigate with magnifying glasses. The construction of a pond with the local wildlife group helped the children discover pond life, finding tadpoles, frogs and dragonflies for the first time. Old pipes, guttering and bricks donated by a large DIY shop were used for building structures. An area of grasses, bamboo and shiny objects like old CD discs and old cutlery, which the children had collected and hung on trees, created a listening area for sounds. Some fundraising events by parents bought a musical

(Continued)

(Continued)

mushroom for children to sit under, listening to the nursery rhymes playing from it. A box of musical instruments for children to play, shake and bang completed the listening area in the outdoor space. The area is evolving all the time; we asked the children what they would like in the outdoor space – they wanted a tree house. Following an appeal, the local wood yard donated some planks of wood, and staff and parents are now building a tree house for the children to play and hide in.

Questions for reflection: creating an outdoor space

Identify an outdoor space that young children spend time in; reflect on the environment as a space to enable exploration and learning:

- How enabling is the environment?
- What resources are there for children to explore and develop knowledge and understanding about the world?
- How can the environment be developed to facilitate further exploration and discovery?

The man-made urban environment also provides a source for exploration and discovery (Shirley, 2010). While sitting in the Peace Gardens in Sheffield, I watched children running into, out of and under the fountains of water shooting up from the ground, laughing as they explored the properties of water and discovering the joy of playing in it. Without opportunities to explore, children have limited knowledge of man-made and living materials and their properties and possibilities for use. Wyse (2004) argues that exploration allows children to develop their knowledge, skills and understanding, and to progress to more creative or conventional responses.

Exploratory learning

Provision for children under 3 years is an area of practice becoming more important as younger children attend early years settings. The provision of developmentally appropriate activity to suit each child's individual needs through relevant pedagogy is key to providing an environment for exploratory learning. An educator or teacher working with young children is a facilitator of open-ended resources that babies and very young children can explore through play (Holland, 2010). Play as high-level activity, like learning, is developmental. Epistemic play behaviour, as defined by Hutt et al. (1989), concerns exploration, discovery, the acquisition of knowledge and skills and problem solving. Adults need to support and encourage children in exploratory play, and through observation, find ways to extend play and discovery with little adult intervention, except for friendly interchanges of gestures and verbal comments (Holland, 2010).

Knowledge of child development is essential for working with young children, so that teachers and educators will have developmentally appropriate expectations of the children in their care. A group of 4-year-olds engaged in a cutting and sticking activity will cut paper into shapes, glue them onto card and make a picture. Babies under 15 months of age will explore the properties of the glue, dripping it from the spreader, and feel the paper's texture. Children become absorbed in pursuing their own exploration of materials (Holland, 2010). Teachers and educators are often concerned with the production of an end product, overlooking the fun, excitement and learning to be gained from the process of exploring materials. Heuristic and treasure basket play, in which the adult is a resource provider and an observer, enables babies and young children to explore materials through their senses.

Heuristic play, devised by Elinor Goldschmied (1987), is exploratory play for children aged 10–20 months, and involves filling empty containers with objects. The adult provides a variety of good quality objects like empty tins, jar lids, woollen pom-poms, wooden clothes pegs, metal and wooden curtain rings, metal chains and ping pong balls. The exploration of materials and the discovery of the materials' properties aid young children's understanding of the mathematical concepts of capacity, shape, size and area.

Treasure basket play, developed by Goldschmied and Hughes (1986) for seated babies aged 4–9 months, offers a basket of natural objects like fir cones, pebbles, shells, pumice, corks, driftwood, apples, oranges and lemons and wooden objects like spoons, pegs, pastry brushes, raffia ornaments and wooden coasters. These baskets of varied and attractive objects allow babies to manipulate and explore materials in a sensory way (Parker-Rees, 2010), aiding mathematical understanding of shape and size. Heuristic and treasure basket play enables exploratory observation: young children can begin to classify objects according to specific criteria like shape, size and texture. As Gascoyne (2012) points out, this exploration is the start of scientific learning.

Outdoor learning spaces

The natural world offers a wealth of sensory experiences and open-ended materials to explore. Experiences in outdoor play spaces provide opportunities for nurturing children's health and well-being and lessening aggressive behaviours (Wilson, 2012). The outdoor environment is central to education and care in Denmark and other Nordic countries as it contributes to the well-being of children socially and physically. Primary-aged children in Norway spend 20 per cent of their time outdoors, playing in the snow, exploring materials in the natural environment and taking more risks than children in the UK, such as whittling sticks with knives, cooking on open fires, climbing rocks and trees (Springate and Foley, 2008). Children in Denmark will have a wilder outdoor experience than children in the UK due to cultural and geographical differences (Knight, 2013), such as the Danish interests in skiing, hiking and cooking outdoors.

The recognition and value of outdoor play are growing, particularly through the forest school pedagogy of learning outdoors, based on an approach used in Scandinavian countries, where the forest is seen as an outdoor learning space. The forest school pedagogy of outdoor learning has influenced many schools and early years settings in England, Wales and Scotland (Knight, 2013; Waters, 2013); here teachers regularly take children to woodland areas where they can take risks, explore, walk, run, jump, swing, paddle, look, smell, see, collect and build (Hallet, 2014), engaging in play-based scientific learning about the natural world and living things.

Problem solving, investigation and enquiry

Problem solving, investigation, enquiry and reasoning are integral to mathematical and scientific learning. Mathematics is often perceived as recording with pen and paper, but early mathematical concepts can be learned before the child has the ability to represent maths problems symbolically (Kay, 2002). Most people think of mathematics as arithmetic, number and calculation (Montague-Smith and Price, 2012), yet Devlin (2003) defines maths as the study of pattern; these may be patterns in number as in algebra, in shape or in spatial position. We make sense of the world by looking for patterns, understanding people through patterns of behaviour and understanding the natural world through patterns of season and cycles of growth. For children to become confident and competent users of mathematics, they should recognize that it can help solve problems and identify recurring patterns and themes (Pound, 2001).

Like literacy, mathematics is a life skill: we use mathematical knowledge and understanding and skills when shopping, to count money; in cooking, to measure, weigh, estimate and time the cooking process; in driving, to read the speedometer and the petrol gauge when filling the car with petrol; in daily functions like inputting a bank PIN number, using a calculator, checking a raffle ticket. There are specific mathematical concepts and associated language, such as up, under, size, shape, adding up, taking away, dividing, fractions. Under Mathematics in the EYFS curriculum (DfE, 2014a), children are expected to use everyday language to talk about mathematical concepts, solve problems, recognize, create and describe patterns and use mathematical language to describe and calculate.

For children to achieve this, they must develop mathematical knowledge and understanding through real and meaningful contexts so that they develop a disposition to enjoy learning maths. The teacher has a significant role to play in developing this learning disposition (Pound, 2001), as young children's future ability to think mathematically depends on the experiences, social interactions and accompanying language that children meet in their formative years. Research in New Zealand by Young-Loveridge (2008) found that children who do best in mathematics on entry to school usually come from families where number has a clear and visible focus in their day-to-day lives. Maths can be included in everyday activities: parents counting the stairs when carrying their child to bed; counting pairs of cutlery when laying the table; counting how many places are set at the table; in making a cake, weighing ingredients.

Contextualizing mathematical learning and providing for real and purposeful inquiry is at the centre of mathematical learning (Tucker, 2014). When a child begins school, their experience of mathematics goes from the meaningful to the abstract very quickly, and bridging the gap between 'real' and 'school' maths can be difficult (Carruthers and Worthington, 2011). Teachers and educators need to provide experiences through which children can make connections and see a purpose in solving problems (Tucker, 2014). Opportunities in everyday routines and experiences include counting votes for the most and least popular lunch preferences of the day, finding out how many children attended school, and how many more or fewer than yesterday (Tucker, 2014). These opportunities enable adults to model mathematical language, show the process of problem solving and support children's thinking and inquiry with questions: What if? Why did that happen?

Within an enabling environment of child-initiated learning, adults have a key role to play in providing children with the opportunity and means to explore, question and investigate the world around them. Investigation, inquiry and questioning are central to becoming scientifically literate, which concerns being able to interpret ideas about the world around you, using the scientific knowledge and evidence you already have (Peacock and Dunne, 2015). Science, as defined by Peacock and Dunne (2015), concerns testing ideas against evidence, mostly through the senses and reliable measurements. Science is a process of enquiry rather than a list of facts. First-hand activities allow children to experience science in real-life contexts, such as an activity where children plant different types of bulbs in bowls; as they observe, measure and record growth, they are collecting and handling data, making predictions about which bulb will bloom first.

Play-based science

Play-based science, as defined by Hoskins (2015), is activity that focuses on play within science, supporting early science exploration within everyday settings. Exploratory early years science is intrinsically linked to play as play starts with children's exploration of materials in their environment (Siraj-Blatchford and MacLeod-Brudenell, 1999). There are strong links between children's natural tendency to play and the best practices of science learning (Kanter et al., 2011). Through exploratory and investigative play, children engage in high-quality science investigations due to the decision-making processes they experience (Forbes and McCloughan, 2010). The flexibility and open-ended nature of play-based science present different options for learning; the process enables children to choose and develop ownership of and agency around the direction of exploration (Hoskins, 2015). In a playful environment, children develop specific scientific process skills: observing, communicating, predicting, planning, investigating, classifying, experimenting, changing variables, understanding cause and effect, and forming conclusions (Pramling and Pramling-Samuelsson, 2001: 73). The following story of practice illustrates examples of play-based science provision and practice.

Story of practice: play-based science

Reema is an early years teacher with responsibility for curriculum development in her nursery. She is leading a series of staff development meetings about using play to develop children's scientific knowledge, understanding and skills. At last week's meeting, as a group they developed a spider chart of play-based science activities. At this week's staff meeting, Reema sets out some of the play-based science activities in the nursery for staff to experience: a sand tray, with containers of small-world figures, mini-beasts, dinosaurs, fir cones and shells on a table beside it; a water tray with containers and tubes; a tray of gloop, a tray of flour, different-coloured playdough; an investigative area with light bulbs, batteries and connectors. At the end of the session, Reema asks staff to write down what they have learned about science during their play. These experiences of play-based science were used as a starting point for discussion and consideration of how to further develop play-based science within the provision. Following the discussion, Reema wrote an information leaflet summarizing how play-based science provision enables children's scientific learning and development of science skills. The leaflet included suggestions of first-hand activities for staff to use with children.

Play-based science provision and practice

Adapted from Hoskins (2015: 74–80):

Sand and water play provides knowledge and understanding about floating and sinking. Exploring a variety of objects and their attributes, like rough, smooth, hard, soft, enables sorting and classifying. The activities of sifting, funnelling, sinking, floating and classifying will feature in later learning in science. Key to keeping children interested in sand and water play is to regularly change the resources and approaches: refreshing the sand and water tray by changing the water's colour, temperature or smell; changing objects using themes – natural objects (shells, pebbles, fir cones), small-world objects (people and animals) or a colour theme (all objects are the same colour).

Messy play offers children the opportunity to explore the properties of materials. As children work with mixtures such as gloop, custard, mousse, dough and mud, they will begin to mix, stir, squish, squash, squeeze, pull, twist, flatten and roll. As they manipulate materials, children learn about materials and their properties and develop conceptual knowledge and understanding about forces.

Investigative area

An investigative area builds on the traditional nature table of collections of seasonal items, like autumn leaves. An investigative area has specific scientific resources and equipment that children can access independently and safely at all times. Resources follow a specific science theme – for example, various sizes of magnets, along with objects of different plastic, metal and fabric materials, for the theme 'magnetic exploration'. Children investigate which objects and materials are attracted to a magnet and which are not. Through exploratory play with magnets and materials, children learn about forces and the properties of materials.

Role-play

Socio-dramatic role-play can help children come to terms with potentially stressful situations, like going to the dentist or visiting the doctor. Children will often play with a stethoscope or x-ray images and pretend to be a doctor, nurse or vet acting out authentic tasks within the job role. Through play, children understand aspects of medical science related jobs and develop emotional resilience to everyday medical experiences.

Small-world play

Children's small-world lorries, cars, tractors and other vehicles enable them to explore how things move by pushing and pulling. Playing with small-world toys like plastic animals can begin thinking about what animals look like and what natural habitat they live in. Opportunities for children to focus on animal habitats can be created. A shallow tray filled with water and plastic pond creatures or toy plastic animals like penguins and polar bears in a tray of ice cubes and snow for children to play with, lays the foundations for further teaching and learning about animals and their habitats within the primary National Curriculum, Key Stage 1.

(Continued)

(Continued)

Outdoor play

The best classroom and the richest cupboard are roofed only by the sky. (McMillan, 1914, cited in Beeley, 2012: 31)

The open-endedness and flexibility of the outdoors provide opportunity for a variety of play-based science; interactions with nature, seasons and the weather provide understanding about the natural world. Nature or 'welly walks', where children collect natural resources to use inside an early years setting, like leaves and grasses, sheep's wool to weave with and plants to naturally dye fabrics, help children sort and classify according to specific criteria. The use of multiple environments outside the classroom, including school grounds and the local community, connects learning outside with the inside learning environment.

The adult's role

In play-based science, the adult's role is to facilitate, resource, encourage, support, scaffold and sensitively intervene in children's play-based science, providing children with the opportunities and means to explore, question and investigate the world around them, allowing adequate time and space for children to freely explore and discover.

 Questions for reflection: play-based science

Reflect on Pramling and Pramling-Samuelsson's (2001) thinking about play-based learning (cited in Hoskins, 2015:73):

In a playful environment, children develop specific scientific process skills:

observing, communicating, predicting, planning, investigating, classifying, experimenting, changing variables and concluding.

- In your daily work or on a work placement, describe a play-based science activity that develops one or more of the scientific process skills described above by Pramling and Pramling-Samuelsson.
- How do you know a child is developing scientific knowledge, understanding and skills?
- How can you further develop play-based science provision in your work with children?

Policy and practice in early science and mathematics education

The comparative research study, 'Creative Little Scientists' (CLS), investigates policy and practice in science and mathematics education for children aged 3–8 years and their potential to foster creativity and inquiry learning and teaching in nine European countries: Belgium, France, Finland, Germany, Greece, Malta, Portugal, Romania and the UK (Creative Little Scientists, 2015). Inquiry-based learning is a key part of policy in all countries within the study. Teachers in preschool and early primary science and mathematics referred to inquiry-based learning and activities associated with observation, questioning, communication and the use of simple tools. They valued pedagogical approaches that promoted dialogue and collaboration in science amongst children and learning approaches based on building on children's prior experiences or relating science and mathematics to everyday life. The majority of teachers in all the European countries used playful exploration as appropriate pedagogy for pre-school children's mathematical and scientific learning. Teachers and policy guidance promoted learning and teaching approaches linked to developing children's problem solving and agency, questioning and curiosity, reflection and reasoning (CLS, 2015: 16).

Teachers viewed themselves as facilitators of children's inquiry, using scaffolding as learning and teaching pedagogy, delaying instruction until the child had opportunity to investigate and inquire on their own or with others. In both preschool and primary settings, rich motivating contexts for play and exploration fostered opportunities for the generation of ideas, and purposes for inquiry were linked to children's everyday experiences, allowing scope for children's decision making. Dialogue and collaboration promoted the use of group work and teacher questioning, encouraging the processes of reflection and explanation associated with the evaluation of ideas and strategies. The important use of sensitive and responsive teacher scaffolding to support independence and extend inquiry, particularly when to intervene or when to stand back to listen and observe and build on children's development of their ideas and questions, was highlighted (CLS, 2015).

The research study recorded many episodes of children's mathematical and scientific learning in a range of first-hand activities: making musical instruments, exploring magnetic attraction, measuring outside. Children were observing and making connections, questioning, explaining evidence and communicating explanations. Children's inquiry skills and understandings noted in the episodes were interconnected with a number of creative attributes. Children were motivated and curious to come up with something new, and therefore asked questions while actively exploring and investigating. Children showed a sense of initiative and a growing ability to collaborate in deciding what to do in carrying out investigations. Children showed imagination, an ability to make connections, and thinking skills in offering explanations.

The Creative Little Scientists (2015), a research study on early science and mathematics education found across the nine European countries, has a common emphasis on the importance of play, exploration and investigation and the promotion of curiosity and thinking skills in policy and in teachers' practice.

Implications for practice

A flexible playful pedagogy to provision and practice encouraging discovery, exploratory and child-centred play is more effective in developing inquiring children than didactic, controlling approaches that adversely affect behaviour and motivation for learning.

Moyles' (2010: 8) view considers children's exploratory learning for developing knowledge and understanding about the world. Pedagogy and practice to enable children's exploration, investigation and inquiry have implications for the role of practitioners, educators and teachers. They become resource providers and facilitators of flexible, open-ended indoor and outdoor contexts. By allowing time for children to explore, supporting, scaffolding and enabling children's exploratory learning through sensitive intervention and questioning, they further children's understanding, investigation and discovery of the world around them.

 ## Further reading

Level 4

Knight, S. (ed.) (2013) *International perspectives on forest school: natural spaces to play and learn*. London: Sage.
This book considers forest school and related approaches to learning outdoors used nationally and internationally.

Level 5

Franzen, K. (2014) 'Under-threes' mathematical learning: teachers' perspectives', *Early Years*, 34 (3) 241–54.
This journal article concerns research on pre-school children's mathematical learning undertaken in Sweden.

Level 6

Mawson, W.B. (2014) 'Experiencing the "wild woods": the impact of pedagogy on children's experience of a natural environment', *European Early Childhood Research Journal*, 22 (4) 513–24.
This journal article describes how teachers' differing pedagogical approaches to 'the wild woods', a nearby wooded natural environment, impacted on children's experiences.

NCTL Teachers' Standards (Early Years)

Standard 3.5

- Demonstrate a clear understanding of appropriate strategies in the teaching of early mathematics.

Tucker, K. (2014) *Mathematics through play in the early years* (3rd edn). London: Sage.
This book provides comprehensive knowledge about the teaching of mathematics through play, grounded in research, policy and practice.

Part 3
Joined-up Early Years Practice

Introduction

The four chapters in Part 3 discuss four themes that join up early years practice. As pedagogical approaches to professional practice, they inform and underpin practitioners', educators' and teachers' work with children, families and other professionals. Like sewing thread, these pedagogical approaches join the patchwork squares of early years practice together, making a patchwork quilt that becomes a cloak of professional practice for practitioners, educators and teachers in their daily working practices with young children and families.

Chapter 9, 'Partnership practice with parents and families', considers working in partnership with parents, carers and families and their key role in their child's early education in settings, schools and the home learning environment. The transition from home to school and the facilitation of a smooth transitional process for children and parents are explored.

Chapter 10, 'Inclusive early years practice', examines the cross-curricular pedagogy of equality and diversity for inclusive practice in working with children, parents and families. Inclusive education by enabling equal access to the curriculum for children with special educational needs is discussed within an agenda of social justice.

Chapter 11, 'Researching early years practice', explores the importance of researching early years practice to inform and impact on professional practice and influence national policy from an evidence base. Becoming and being a researcher are discussed through autobiographical reflective enquiry, and ways to share and disseminate research are considered.

Chapter 12, 'Leading early years practice', explores the phenomenon of early years leadership within the context of professional leadership development. Government policy concerning the development of a workforce of graduate leaders through higher educational professional awards and the development of leadership roles is examined. A model of early years leadership developed from research is explored to consider leadership styles and practices.

Throughout these chapters, the practitioner's, educator's and teacher's role in providing joined-up early years practice is considered. Each chapter concludes with reflective consideration of implications for practice. *Stories of practice* provide examples of real-life practice, while *Questions for reflection* provide opportunities for reflection on the four themes in joined-up early years practice. Suggestions for further reading at the end of each chapter signpost the reader to other resources on the themes and issues discussed.

Chapter 9

Partnership Practice with Parents and Families

Chapter overview

This chapter considers working in partnership with parents, carers and families and the key role parents have in their child's early education. Effective partnership practice is defined and challenges in developing equality in partnership working examined. Research on effective home learning environments for children's learning and educational achievement is discussed. The issue of transition from home to school, including facilitating a smooth transitional process for parents and children, is explored. Examples of effective partnership practice with parents are given, with reflective questions to prompt reflective thinking. The term 'parents' is used for 'parents, carers and families' throughout the chapter.

Partnership working

Working in partnership with parents is included in the EYFS curriculum document as a key aspect of provision, as parents are seen as key partners in supporting children's learning and development (DCSF, 2008; DfE, 2014a). Parents are a child's first and most significant influence (Beckley, 2012) and should be recognized as children's first and enduring educators (DCSF, 2008). The Plowden Report (CACE, 1967) highlighted the importance of parental involvement in primary children's education. Prior to this report, a red line painted on the school playground prevented parents from stepping over it and into their child's school. Parental engagement is now included in national policy in the UK (England, Scotland, Wales and Northern Ireland) (DfE, 2014b).

The term 'partnership' is used frequently when working with parents to reflect parental involvement, participation and engagement and can range from attending parents' evenings, being a member of a school's parent–teacher association, being part of the playgroup management team as a committee member, or, in school management, being a parent–school governor, to collaboration in the learning process and the curriculum. Working in partnership with parents is interpreted in a number of ways (Beckley, 2012; Draper and Duffy, 2010); these can include parents working with staff and children in settings and schools, teachers visiting families in their homes, parents attending workshops or courses, and parents running services such as a toy library. On a continuum of involvement, parents' engagement ranges from reading a newsletter to becoming a valued member of the partnership team.

Partnership concerns effective relationships; Whalley (2007) defines a true partnership, recognizing a sharing of practice on equal terms. A 'triangle of care' between parents, professionals and children in the *Start Right* report (Ball, 1994) described a new kind of equal and active partnership between parents and professionals. Parents' skills, competences and commitment to their children's learning were recognized. Partnership goes beyond involvement (Foot et al., 2002) – it is not just about parents merely helping and information sharing, but partnership implies an equality of power that includes parents in decision-making and policy issues.

When parents and practitioners work together in early years settings, the results have a positive impact on children's development and learning (Beckley, 2012). Research studies demonstrate this: the Peers Early Education Partnership (PEEP) project (1995–2005) found lasting benefits for children from birth to starting school; the EPPE (1997–2003) study identified that the home learning environment provided by parents plays a key role in children's educational achievements; and research by the Centre for Excellence and Outcomes (C4EO, 2010) highlighted how families influence children's learning.

Good relationships with professionals benefit parents and families as they know and understand what their child is doing in the setting or school; develop further knowledge and understanding of child development, provision and practice; help them feel valued and respected; and contribute to the setting or school. Effective partnership working with parents is developed through trust, sharing decision making, responsibility and accountability (Draper and Duffy, 2010). There can be challenges to developing this partnership (Hurst and Joseph, 2010). Parents may have negative memories of their education at school, they may perceive teachers to be the expert, there may be a lack of shared language and working patterns may not fit into the school day, making it difficult to participate in setting or school-based activities.

Research on parental involvement shows that parents want to have their views considered and to be listened to, respected and treated as partners in the upbringing of their children (Ghate and Hazel, 2001; Quinton, 2004). However, partnerships may not necessarily be equal (Hurst and Joseph, 2010). There may also be challenges for practitioners working together in partnership with parents. They may lack confidence in working with parents, especially if they are newly or recently qualified. If practitioners, educators or teachers regard themselves as experts on children's learning, they may have difficulty in valuing parents' views and parenting practices.

Draper and Duffy (2010: 272) describe partnership practice with parents in their setting, the Thomas Coram Children's Centre in London, identifying that a successful partnership involves a two-way flow of information, flexibility and responsiveness:

> We want to create a centre that reflects our ethos that everyone is welcome, that parents can express their views and feelings, that diversity is valued and that the centre is seen as part of the wider community.

Partnership for them is centred on four aspects of practice:

- working with parents around children's learning
- support for parents
- access to further training
- parental involvement in management.

Working with parents

There has been a long tradition of working with parents in early childhood settings; until the 1960s parental involvement programmes were used for children with low achievement, compensating for the limitations of the home. Recently, models of parental involvement have shifted from the compensatory to the participatory (Draper and Duffy, 2010), moving away from the 'we know best' model of parental involvement of support and intervention to a model of parental collaboration in children's learning (Whalley, 2007). This involves encouraging parents to participate and collaborate with professionals (Reed and Murphy, 2012). The Nutbrown Review (2012) of early years education and childcare qualifications recommends that practitioners regard parents as experts on their own children, and that they listen and learn from them so as to support each child's well-being, learning and development. As experts on their child and family's cultural heritage, parents are a resource to embrace (Draper and Duffy, 2010). Children's life at home provides opportunities for learning which the setting or school can build on, as the following story of practice shows.

Story of practice: Chinese cooking

Lee had recently moved into the area from China and found settling into school difficult. He was learning English as his second language and finding the noise and culture of his primary school different and overwhelming; even the food at lunchtime was different to his usual diet. Zara, his teacher, was concerned: how could she help him settle in and feel more at home? As Chinese New Year approached, she wanted to include the celebration in her practice. She knew Lee's mother liked cooking at home and asked her if she would like to come and cook some traditional Chinese food for the children in her class. So, one afternoon, Lee's mum became a cookery demonstrator and Lee her helper, cooking fluffy rice and lemon chicken for the children, with Chinese music playing in the background. The food was shared; each child had a bowl of rice, a piece of lemon chicken and great fun in eating it with chopsticks. Lee handed out the fortune cookies his mum had made, one to each child; Lee helped to read the messages inside, written in Chinese. To finish the Chinese-themed afternoon, Lee's grandfather played music on his liuqin, a small lute that the children listened to.

In the days after the cooking session, Zara noticed that the children were talking, playing and engaging more with Lee, who was now smiling and playing with the children. The cooking session had helped the children know more about Lee's family and cultural heritage, and Lee felt he had been recognized and valued as a child in his class, becoming more confident. Zara developed the topic of Chinese New Year in follow-up activities: the children wrote their own messages in fortune cookies, giving them to their friends in the class, and they made cards for their families to celebrate the Chinese festival. Zara also contacted the local Chinese community who performed a traditional Lion Dance for the children, prompting them to make Chinese lions from recycled boxes, decorated with paint and collage materials.

Questions for reflection: Chinese cooking

Referring to the story of practice above, reflect on the benefits of working with parents:

- How has the Chinese cooking activity benefitted the children in Lee's class?
- How has the Chinese cooking activity benefitted Lee?
- How has the Chinese cooking activity benefitted Lee's mother?
- How has the Chinese cooking activity benefitted Lee's teacher?

Home learning environment

A major research question for the EPPE 3–11 research study investigated whether children's home learning experiences could reduce social inequalities. The quality of the home learning environment (HLE) was identified as the most significant factor in predicting children's learning outcomes when other background factors were taken into account (Siraj-Blatchford, 2010b). The quality of the HLE, where parents actively engaged in activities with children, strongly promoted intellectual and social development in children. Those with a low HLE gained an advantage from attending any pre-school, and particularly a higher quality pre-school. Disadvantaged children therefore needed both a strong HLE and a high-quality pre-school (Sylva et al., 2007). Seven types of home-learning activities were found to be especially significant:

- the frequency of being read to
- going to the library
- playing with numbers
- painting and drawing
- being taught letters
- being taught numbers
- being taught songs, poems and rhymes.

The EPPE research found that a wide range of family members provided support for children's learning, including parents, sisters and brothers, aunts, uncles, grandparents and cousins. Reading to children and listening to children read was the most frequent activity (Siraj-Blatchford, 2010b). Reading at home and taking children to the library is seen as an educational schema (Giddens, 1984) used by middle- and working-class parents (Abbas, 2007), and higher levels of early years HLE were predictive of higher participation in all out-of-school activities at the age of 11 years.

Families tend to make the extra efforts required in developing a rich HLE when they believe these efforts will be rewarded, and when parents are aware that their child has the potential to succeed and they recognize that they have an active role to play in realizing this potential and that social disadvantages may be overcome (Siraj-Blatchford, 2010b).

The demographics of the family are not static as society and the way we live changes. Throughout Europe, the number of children born outside marriage has increased, there is greater recognition of same-sex relationships and, due to family economics, grandparents now undertake more childcare (Reed and Murphy, 2012). Research by Flouri and Buchanan (2004) shows that early involvement of fathers and mothers at age 7 independently predicted educational attainment by the age of 20. Not growing up in an intact two-parent family did not weaken the association between father and mother's involvement and educational outcomes in a child's education. The EPPE 3–11 research found that mothers with good qualifications (a degree or higher) were much more likely to have their children take part in sports and arts activities, and private music lessons, than those below degree level.

Parental interest and involvement are only 'visible' in most educational settings when parents are in the nursery, early years setting or school premises, helping in the classroom with routine chores, hearing children read, fund-raising, attending meetings. Parents away from the educational setting make a large 'invisible' investment in the home environment (Brooker, 2008). Parents read bedtime stories; help their child read packaging, pictorial and written logos and labels when shopping; float plastic letters in the bath to make words; and demonstrate reading and writing by answering emails on their laptop, searching for information on the internet, reading newspapers, catalogues and books (Hallet, 2008). Building on home experiences and valuing parents' contribution strengthen home–school links, particularly when children start school.

Transition to school

Bronfenbrenner (1979) describes transition as a change in location or environment and a change of role and identity or both. As humans grow, they experience a process of differing transitions throughout their life's journey (Brooker, 2012):

- *life changes* – e.g. growing up, maturing, parenting, ageing
- *family changes* – involving parents, step-parents, siblings, reconstituted families
- *care changes* – e.g. moving from one caregiver to another
- *educational changes* – e.g. moving from one educational establishment to another
- *starting school and moving to another school* – moving from the familiarity of the home and setting or school environment to a new and unfamiliar locale.

Successive changes can impact on young children's stress, separation and insecure attachments, affecting not only a child's emotional health but also their cognitive development (O'Conner, 2013). Transition describes a change in a child's identity and a threat to the child's sense of well-being (Brooker, 2012). Adults involved in children's lives help children get used to new people and places, and support their well-being and emotional health by developing emotional resilience for change (O'Conner, 2013).

Starting school is a major transition not only for children but for parents too. Practitioners, educators and teachers should 'think child' (Rhodes, 2008) when trying to understand the change from a home setting with familiar surroundings, routines and carers to an unfamiliar environment of routines and educarers. The following story of practice illuminates aspects of a child's first day at school from a child's perspective.

Story of practice: starting school

I could see two tables in a huge room. These were really big tables and I heard someone say that they 'provide a focus for learning'. One was called 'the creative table'; it was near lots of paper, empty egg boxes, drinking straws and cardboard boxes, paint and brown stuff which some of the children were sticking their fingers into, getting themselves really messy. There was one child with a really funny name; they kept calling him 'Apron Tom, Apron Tom' till he put on an old shirt; then they seemed to be much happier.

I walked over to another part of the room where a woman said children could do 'fine manipulation and skills of construction'. That was silly; all I saw were lego and bricks. There was a place with lots of books where you could sit down. There were doors to the outside, but I did not want to go out there. I wanted to play on the carpet with toys ...

Questions for reflection: starting school

- Continue the story, providing a child's view of a first day at school.
- Consider what things she might find strange compared to home.
- What if English was not her first language – how would she feel, how would she engage in the activities?
- If you were using this story to help explain to parents what it must be like to be at school for the first time, what other issues could you introduce and why?

Starting school is a significant milestone in a child's life, described by Brooker (2008: 25) as a 'vertical transition', where a child 'steps up' the educational ladder from pre-school to the next stage of schooling. Although this is probably not the first time a child has been away from home, as they may have attended nursery, playgroup or daycare, transition into full-time schooling is the beginning of their progress through the education system. Starting school can cause anxiety for a child. What will playtime be like? Can I play with my friend? What will my teacher be like? Will the work be hard?

For a parent, their child starting school is a significant milestone in their life as a parent; their child is leaving their care at home and stepping into the wider world to interact with teachers and educators who influence their child's learning and development. Parents too may experience anxiety around the different routines from those in the home, due to the large number of children in school. Will the teacher know she does not like milk? Will she be rushed to eat her lunch, as she is a slow eater? Will she be able to sit by her friend?

Bowlby's (1969) attachment theory demonstrates the significance of the mother as a key attachment for a child's well-being. Parting and separating can be an anxious time for both child and parent; individuals handle it in different ways due to the family's context and culture and the place of the child in the family (Nutbrown and Page, 2008). At times of transition and separation, parents and children will need reassurance and sensitivity (O'Conner, 2013). The key person approach addresses separation and transition in caregiving, as a designated person works closely with a child and their parent, building a relationship of effective communication, information and care. A travelling key group (Lindon, 2010), where a key person moves with their key group of children from one class to another, offers continuity for children and families. The use of transitional objects (Winnicott, 1953), which are favoured toys or objects such as a comfort blanket, links the security of a familiar home environment with the unfamiliar pre-school or school. Winnicott describes transition for a child as much more than being separated from their parent in a physical sense; it is also a growing awareness in the child that they are separate from their parent and a person in their own right.

Parental and school expectations

Parents have expectations of the school and teachers have expectations of parents. Parents' own experiences of school influence the way they prepare their children for school and bring them to the classroom for the first time (Brooker, 2002), and also how they engage in the life of the school and their child's education.

The Tickell Review of the EYFS (2011) recommends further emphasis on the role of parents in their children's learning and for practitioners to include effective parental engagement in their practice. The pedagogic discourse of schools, including policy on parental involvement, describes the school's expectations of parents. When their child starts school, parents have to learn how to be a 'good school parent' (Brooker, 2002). The successful parent provides school-like activities at home, takes their child to school regularly and on time, supports their child and teacher in the classroom and attends all parents' meetings and school performances (Brooker, 2002). Teachers usually welcome the involvement of parents who support their teacher's practice and the school's pedagogy, not those who contest school policies and practices (Vincent, 1996).

The notion of school readiness in England's national policy (Tickell, 2011) emphasizes the role of parents and teachers in supporting their child in transition to school. In her review of the EYFS, Tickell (2011) considers school readiness in the light of school un-readiness, and a school being ready for children. Children who are toilet trained, have adequate sleep in a regular sleep pattern, can dress independently, and are able to listen to and socialize with other children, will have beneficial experiences of school, while children without these skills may be hindered in their learning. Children being school-ready, that is, ready to engage in a formal learning environment, highlights the contribution of parenting to children's comfortable transition to a more educational context of schooling.

Scaffolding transition

Starting school is a key experience for children, parents and families. The role of relationships in early transitions into educational settings is central for a smooth transition process for parent, child and teacher, such as from pre-school to school. Pianta and Cox (1999) describe this transition as a process of relationship formation, establishing a relationship between the home and the school in which the child's development is the key focus. A close relationship between the child and parents is crucial to successful transitions into 'the world beyond the familiar one' (Hurst and Joseph, 2010: 261). Mutually beneficial relationships between parents, practitioners, educators and teachers should underpin children's care and learning (Jackson and Needham, 2014). Most nurseries, settings and schools use some strategies for scaffolding the transition process (Brooker, 2012), through which beneficial relationships for parents, the child and teachers are established, as shown in the following story of practice.

Story of practice: transition programme

Alan is the head teacher of an infant school; there is a nursery in a separate building on the school site. As a child, when he started school, parents were not allowed to go into school and only entered when summoned by the head teacher with concerns about their child. On his first day at school, he was literally left at the school gate to enter an unfamiliar space of adults, children and objects. Drawing on this experience, he wanted a more welcoming school start for parents, as he believed an informed parent affects their child's disposition to learning and school life. He appointed a nursery liaison teacher to lead a transition programme in the term before the children started school. The programme included a home visit and a series of meetings for parents and families. Through these meetings, a two-way process of information sharing and relationship building developed.

Bluebell school

Transition programme: meetings for parents and families

Each meeting has a theme for information sharing, with time for questions from parents and families:

- **Home visit**

The child's class teacher and the nursery liaison teacher visit the child in the familiar surroundings of their home with their caregiver(s) for the purposes of relationship building and information gathering, such as in relation to dietary needs.

- **Meeting 1 – *Starting school***

The first meeting takes place with the head teacher in the familiar context of the nursery, explaining the purpose of the transition programme, which is to provide a continuity of education and care for children starting school.

- **Meeting 2 – *Early learning***

The second meeting involves the liaison teacher and teachers in the reception class. Talk and discussion are led by the teachers on children's early learning, the EYFS as a curriculum framework for learning and ways of working with children in school. Parents are invited to participate in the literacy, mathematical, science, art and play activities their child will experience, followed by a discussion about how these activities enable children's learning.

- Meeting 3 – *Parental involvement*

The third meeting is hosted by existing parents and parent governors in the parents' room in school, who explain ways of being involved in the school – as a helper in the classroom and on school trips; organizing refreshments for the monthly birthday assembly; working with your child in the language workshop; borrowing books, games and story DVDs to use at home; as a fundraiser in the parent–teacher association; or on the school board as a parent-governor.

 Questions for reflection: transition practices

Reflect on transition practices in your work setting or work placement. Write down the activities in place for parents in your school or setting:

- before transition to school or pre-school
- after their child starts school or pre-school.

How do these transition practices benefit:

- parents?
- children?
- teachers?

What more could the setting or school do to support transitions?

Implications for practice

Strong partnerships between parents and teachers can only prove to be advantageous for the children concerned. These help children feel secure in a strange environment so that experiences can build on experiences gained at home and in the community. Positiveness, sensitivity, responsiveness and friendliness can all be demonstrated through effective communication and form a central element of establishing and maintaining effective partnerships with parents and families.

(Continued)

(Continued)

This view by Fitzgerald (2004: 13) draws together issues on the importance of partnership practice with parents for children and ways of developing effective partnership working. For practitioners, educators and teachers to develop strong parental partnerships has implications for practice. Effective partnership practice is built on relationships and communication that take time to develop for the benefits of emotional well-being and educational outcomes that are realized by parents, children, and teachers. When children start school, establishing mutually beneficial relationships with parents and giving children time for transition practices, should be the priorities for teachers.

 ## Further reading

Level 4

Hurst, V. and Joseph, J. (2010) 'Parents and practitioners', in C. Cable, L. Miller and G. Goodliff (eds) *Working with children in the early years* (2nd edn). Abingdon: Routledge.
This chapter discusses an inclusive approach to partnership working with parents for children's emotional well-being and early learning.

Level 5

Brooker, L. (2002) *Starting school: young children's learning cultures*. Buckingham: Open University Press.
Through a case study of an inner-city school, the book addresses key questions about starting school for children and families with differing cultural heritages.

Level 6

Nueum, M. and Nueum, D.L. (2010) 'Parental strategies to scaffold emergent writing skills in pre-school children within the home environment', *Early Years*, 30 (1) 79–94.
This journal article describes how joint-writing activities between parent and child in the home can enhance literacy skills in young children.

NCTL Teachers' Standards (Early Years)

Standard 2.7
- Understand the important influence of parent/carers, working in partnership with them to support children's well-being and development.

Draper, L. and Duffy, B. (2010) 'Working with parents', in C. Cable, L. Miller and G. Goodliff (eds) *Working with children in the early years* (2nd edn). Abingdon: Routledge.
The authors of this chapter describe their partnership practice with parents, examining the benefits of partnership working for children, parents and teachers.

Standard 5.4
- Support children through a range of transitions.

O'Conner, A. (2013) *Understanding transitions in the early years: supporting change through attachment and resilience*. Abingdon: Routledge.
This book explains why transitions matter and provides practical guidance on how to support young children's developing emotional resilience and management of life changes.

Chapter 10

Inclusive Early Years Practice

Chapter overview

This chapter examines cross-curricular pedagogy of equality and diversity for inclusive practice in working with children, parents and families. The notion of diversity, similarity and difference is explored through examining cultural, language, social and family influences. Adults' values and beliefs as potential barriers for children's learning are considered. Inclusive education, by enabling equal access to the curriculum for children with special educational needs, is discussed. The concept of making every child matter forms a discussion about policy and practice within an agenda of social justice. There is opportunity to reflect on inclusive practice and consider your own inclusive pedagogy and practice.

Diversity

'A unique child' as a principle of practice in the EYFS curriculum (DfE, 2014a) highlights the individual strengths and attributes of a young child and the diversity of children, parents and families with differing cultural heritages, family structure, gender, ability, social and economic status. A range of diverse cultural, linguistic, social and familial factors influences the needs of children in education and care, as shown vertically in Table 10.1 (adapted from Hendry, 2012: 94).

Table 10.1   Diverse influences

Cultural	Language	Social	Family
Country of origin	Children learning English as an additional language	Parental education and literacy	Looked-after children
Experience of education/ school elsewhere	Multilingual or monolingual families	Economic status	Adopted children
		Unemployed parents or on a low income	Prisoners' children
Religion	Literate or non-literate family members		Same-sex parents
Dietary requirements	Newly arrived families or established in the UK	Working parents using childcare	Single parents
			Divorced parents
		Refugees' experience of trauma and living in temporary accommodation	

Ensuring that all children are included and learn to value one another is a challenging aspect of the role for those who work with children and families. It is important for children to make links between their own and others' experiences, to be aware of similarities and differences and to feel a sense of connecting and belonging to their learning community. For children to learn in early years environments, they must feel comfortable, valued and listened to within a framework of boundaries and expectations (Hendry, 2012), and a culture of respectful education (Nutbrown et al., 2013) and social justice that includes children, parents, families and the local community.

In considering diversity and how practitioners, educators and teachers support children's learning, those who work with children should reflect on their own understandings of cultural, language, social and family influences on children's learning and awareness of assumptions and prejudices about race, gender, ability, disability, parenting and social class, which may act as barriers to learning. They should be familiar with children's concepts of themselves, identity and belonging and children's awareness of others' needs, beliefs, similarities and differences (Hendry, 2012). Diversity and difference in the early years setting or school need to be viewed as 'a rich resource to be utilized for the benefit of all, rather than as a problem to be overcome' (Booth et al., 2006: 10). Including diversity in early years practice demands that those who work with children be responsive to the diversity of children and families in their communities (Roberts-Holmes, 2009), by valuing identity and respecting differences in children's learning about themselves and each other. In embracing diversity in inclusive practice, the following questions help to reflect on and shape practice (adapted from Hendry, 2012: 98 and Nutbrown et al., 2013: 16):

- How does each child, parent and family in the setting or school know they are welcomed and respected?
- How do children learn about languages, cultures and ethnic groups that are not represented within the setting or school?
- Is every child in this setting/school seen as equal? Do we treat children equally according to their needs, irrespective of their race, gender, religion, nationality or ability?
- Is every child respected here? Do I say their name correctly? Do I make efforts to know and understand their background and nationality?
- Does every child have their needs met to promote their healthy mental, emotional, cognitive, physical and spiritual development?
- Are children's diverse learning and developmental needs provided for?
- How do we know that our practice is genuinely inclusive and not reinforcing stereotypes?

Inclusive practice as a cross-curricular approach to teaching and learning is the cement between the building blocks of knowledge, as in areas of learning or programmes of study, forming a curriculum wall of learning. Teachers should ensure that all curriculum resources and opportunities for learning throughout the year reflect the diverse and wide range of family backgrounds, multiple languages and faiths (Hendry, 2012). The bi-cultural curriculum, Te Whariki in New Zealand, promotes equality of opportunity in contexts of diversity, through recognizing the link between culture, language and learning (New Zealand Ministry of Education, 1995). The Early Years Learning Framework for Australia: Belonging, Being and Becoming (Australian Government, 2009) recommends that educators recognize and respond to barriers to children achieving educational success, by challenging assumptions and practices that contribute to inequities and making curriculum decisions that promote the inclusion and participation of all children. By developing professional knowledge and skills, working in partnership with children, families, communities, other services and agencies, they endeavour to find equitable and effective ways to ensure that all children have the opportunity to achieve learning outcomes.

Questions for reflection: diversity in inclusive practice

Consider how you include diversity within your practice or observe the inclusion of diversity in practice in your work placement.

Use the questions listed above (Hendry, 2012; Nutbrown et al., 2013) to help you reflect on diversity in inclusive practice:

- How is diversity addressed in practice?
- Can the inclusion of diversity be further developed in practice?

Inclusive education

The concept of inclusion has been defined and used in relation to special educational needs (SEN), however inclusion relates to more than children with SEN and disabilities and also to a philosophical stance of ethical values and beliefs of equality and social justice (Devarakonda, 2013). Inclusive education is about equal opportunities for all, irrespective of age, gender, ethnicity, disability, attainment and background. It gives particular attention to the provision made for the achievement of different groups (Ofsted, 2000). The agenda of inclusive education concerns the overcoming of barriers to participation that may be experienced by children (Ainscow, 1999). Corbett and Slee's (2000) metaphor of integration as the square peg struggling to fit into a round hole illuminates their view of inclusion as a circle containing many shapes of differing sizes within a holistic approach to education. While integration accommodates children, inclusion concerns difference that is celebrated and where every child fits in.

Every early years setting or school presents a culture created by leaders with governors, children, educators, teachers, parents and others. Inclusive processes and practices embedded within this culture, curriculum and services are designed to help all children reach their potential (Nutbrown et al., 2013). The leader of a setting or school with a philosophy of equality and social justice develops with staff an inclusive ethos and culture underpinning inclusive practice, providing appropriate developmental practice to meet the needs of individual children, as illustrated in Figure 10.1.

The government's current school-led agenda of raising attainment through target setting and a discourse of categorizing individual children in terms of attainment create tension between a culture of academic achievement and the development of inclusive practices so that all children may reach their potential

Figure 10.1 Inclusive practice

(Nutbrown et al., 2013). The effects of problematizing difference by identifying children and families 'at risk' offer the potential for difference and exclusion as well as inclusion. Figure 10.2 shows arenas of inclusion/exclusion (adapted from Nutbrown et al., 2013: 9).

Some government strategies promote difference for later educational inclusion. Early intervention, a strategy for working with vulnerable families, aims to support children and families at risk (Allen, 2011). The term 'special educational need' (SEN) is commonly used in the UK to describe a child who has additional need(s) in accessing educational provision. SEN help may be provided in the form of an adult, such as a teaching assistant or learning support assistant working alongside the child in the classroom, or as a physical resource to support a child in writing – for example, a chair to support a child with one arm shorter than the other.

The all-encompassing term 'special educational need' was introduced in the Warnock report (DES, 1978) and subsequent Education Act (1981) to ensure that provision focused on a child's educational needs rather than on non-educational ones (Trussler and Robinson, 2015). This policy promoted an inclusive system of education following the social model of disability, which focuses on the child and the social and life skills needed for independent living. The medical model of disability used prior to the Warnock report focused on the child's condition or illness

Achievement

Age

Challenging behaviour

Disability

Disaffection

Emotional and behavioural difficulty

Employment

Gender

Hearing

Housing

Language

Learning styles

Mental health

Obesity

Physical impairment

Poverty

Race/ethnicity

Religion

Sexual orientation

Sight

Social class

Special educational need

Figure 10.2   Arenas of inclusion/exclusion

and the medical support required for the health of the child (Trussler and Robinson, 2015). The following story of practice demonstrates inclusive education and how through adapting practice to meet an individual child's needs, the child becomes the centre of inclusive educational practice.

Story of practice: inclusive education

Kaila is a Special Educational Needs Co-ordinator (SENCO) in a primary academy working in the Foundation Stage Unit. She describes how she led and supported staff to work with Adam, a 4-year-old boy with speech and language delay:

(Continued)

(Continued)

As SENCO and the child's key person, I had undertaken observations and assessments of Adam in the setting; from these I was able to identify that the child was continually frustrated with the environment, the staff and children due to his language delay, resulting in him being aggressive and displaying low levels of concentration and difficulty in responding to adults' talk and instruction. I was also working with his parents and the speech and language therapist to gather as much information about Adam as possible, to identify strategies they were undertaking so that these could be used in the setting to maintain consistency.

I held a meeting with the Foundation Stage Team to discuss Adam's needs, to confidently share the information I had obtained from other professionals and to enable staff to highlight any issues or difficulties they were experiencing when working with the child. The staff raised issues about what strategies to use, expressing their frustration and lack of confidence in dealing with the situation. From the meeting, I identified that it would be beneficial for the staff to undertake training to meet both their own professional needs and Adam's language needs. I contacted the academy's professional development adviser who signposted me to a short course on communication difficulties, and I asked the facilitator to deliver the course at the academy.

All staff attended the training; they evaluated it as being beneficial to their practice as it was child-focused and practical. The course gave the staff an understanding of how Adam must feel in a situation with limited communication skills, and gave them ways to sensitively approach children with communication difficulty and effective strategies that could be used. As a team, we suggested strategies to use in the setting – these included using a visual timetable, shortening staff language by using clear repeated responses, active listening and modelling language.

Shortly after the strategies were put into place, the staff identified that they were experiencing difficulty in shortening their language responses, so I suggested they observe me whilst I engaged with Adam in a building bricks activity. In turn, each member of staff observed my use of language, then I supported them while they engaged with Adam in another activity. During a feedback session with staff about use of the strategy, they confirmed their confidence was increasing and that they felt more comfortable interacting with Adam due to the strategies provided. This, in turn, increased Adam's concentration levels, his listening skills and language usage; and his aggressive behaviour and frustration were noted to be significantly decreasing. In adapting their communication and interaction with Adam to meet his needs, the adults were putting him at the centre of their practice.

Questions for reflection: inclusive education

Consider an example of inclusive practice that shows how a strategy for learning has been adapted to meet the learning needs of a child:

- Describe the adaptation.
- How did the adaptation benefit the child's learning?
- Can more adaptations be made to encourage the child's further engagement in learning?

Making children matter

As an approach to practice, *Every child matters: change for children* (ECM) (DfES, 2004a) put children and young people from birth to 19 years of age at the centre of provision and practice. An agenda for social justice (Knowles, 2009) for children and young people to achieve well-being in childhood and in later life was the driver for the five outcomes, which were central to ECM policy (DfES, 2004a):

- Be healthy.
- Be safe.
- Enjoy and achieve.
- Make a positive contribution.
- Achieve economic well-being.

Research in a local authority on the implementation of ECM with staff who were practitioners, teachers, leaders and managers from early years settings, primary schools, the youth service, and children and young people's services (Hallet, 2005), found the integrated approach to holistic service delivery provided a common language across service provision. A range of activities emerged from the five ECM outcomes. ECM underscored activities related to health in early years settings and primary schools around healthy eating and cooking; extended school provision through sporting activities; and was embedded in youth service provision – 'it is the basis of our work'/'ECM is the youth service'. Some teachers from primary schools were unclear about the ECM agenda and its aims, 'although planning sheets have ECM tick boxes' to record provision in the classroom. ECM provision was reported in school improvement plans and in the school's self-evaluation for Ofsted. This was reflected in ECM training for leaders and managers who were responsible for reporting ECM provision, although there was a lack of training for practitioners, educators and teachers working with children and families.

The Children's Plan (DCSF, 2007), a 10-year vision built on the ECM agenda, aimed to raise attainment and aspirations for this and future generations of children and young people, and to close gaps in educational achievement, ensuring standards of educational excellence for everyone. ECM developed an integrated service approach to delivery, to health, education and social care professionals working together for better outcomes for children, young people and families. In the view of the DfES (2004a), children cannot learn if they don't feel safe or if health problems are allowed to create barriers, and an education is the most effective route for young children out of poverty and disaffection (DCSF, 2007). Recent reform in the Code of Practice for special educational need provision in England for children and young people from birth to 25 years of age (DfE and DoH, 2015) promotes joint planning and commissioning of services to ensure close co-operation between education, health and social care provision. An Education, Health and Care Plan (EHC) replaces a statement of special educational need for a child, and reflects the integrated service delivery of education, health and social care provision established in the ECM agenda for inclusive practice in settings, schools and further education colleges. EHC plans focus on the holistic development of children and young people.

As stated in the UNCRC (UN, 1989), Article 28, children have a right to an education. They have an entitlement to follow a nationally prescribed curriculum, such as the EYFS or NC. Over the years, educational policy in England, Scotland, Wales and Northern Ireland has developed into a knowledge-based, prescribed, target-led, assessment-focused and adult-led curriculum, but how education is accessed by children is important. The best of early education includes developmentally appropriate practice (DAP), observation-based pedagogy and assessment; close parental involvement; equality of access to a differentiated curriculum; and a multi-professional, cross-agency approach to provision (Nutbrown et al., 2013). Where DAP is used to adapt to children's individual strengths, needs and interests, the notion of special educational needs or additional needs is not required.

Promoting inclusive practice and eliminating discrimination require shared language and understanding by sharing information (Nutbrown et al., 2013). Inclusive practice concerns practitioners', educators' and teachers' role in promoting equality of opportunity and access to the curriculum for all children. The following questions help you to reflect on your values, beliefs and practices in working with children and families in an inclusive way.

 Questions for reflection: inclusive practice

Personal reflection

- Complete the sentence: I believe inclusive practice is ...
- How do I provide access for the children or child I work with?

Professional reflection

- What human and physical resources are provided in my setting or school to make the curriculum accessible to all children?
- How could they be improved?
- Does your setting or school have a policy for special educational needs, equal opportunities or inclusion? Consider why the setting or school has such a policy. What values and beliefs are the drivers for this policy?

Best practice – a child study

- Give an example of effective inclusive practice for a child in your setting, school or work placement.
- What are the key factors in this provision?
- What impact do (or did) they have on the child's learning and development?

Implications for practice

Inclusion in its broadest sense concerns all children, parents, practitioners, educators and teachers in each and every early years community and seeks to demonstrate how inclusive practices can be embedded within early years curriculum, pedagogy and services, which are designed to help all children reach their potential and achieve all that is possible for them.

Nutbrown et al.'s (2013: 16) view defines inclusion as an overarching pedagogy for practice in the care and education of children. This has implications for practice within the changing political agenda of education. Within the ever-increasing climate of assessment, academic achievement, reporting and accountability, it is important to continually remind ourselves of the ethical agenda of inclusion for social justice and equality of opportunity and access when working with children, parents and families.

 Further reading

Level 4

Lambert, S. (2012) 'Inclusion and "educating" the whole child', in P. Beckley (ed.) *Learning in the early years*. London: Sage.

The chapter in this book provides an awareness of inclusion within a holistic approach to children's learning and development.

Level 5

Devarakonda, C. (2013) *Diversity and inclusion in early childhood: an introduction.* London: Sage.
This book provides a clear introduction to what inclusive practice means for those working with children in their earliest years.

Level 6

Trussler, S. and Robinson, D. (2015) *Inclusive practice in the primary school: a guide for teachers.* London: Sage.
This book discusses the challenges teachers face in developing and refining an inclusive classroom.

NCTL Teachers' Standards (Early Years)

Standard 8.1
- Promote equality of opportunity and anti-discriminatory practice.

Nutbrown, C., Clough, P. and Atherton, F. (2013) *Inclusion in the early years* (2nd edn). London: Sage.
This book provides a broad view of inclusion, demonstrating the impact of inclusive practices on children and parents.

Chapter 11

Researching Early Years Practice

Chapter overview

The chapter explores the importance of researching early years practice to inform and impact on professional practice and influence national policy from an evidence base. Becoming and being a researcher are discussed through auto-biographical reflective enquiry, and ways to share and disseminate research are considered. Research enquiry within a framework of action research as an agent for change, work-based reflective learning and understanding the professional self, are discussed. There is opportunity to reflect on examples of research to consider personal and professional learning through the research process and to reflect on the value of researching early years practice.

Personal and professional research stories

Studying on a foundation or undergraduate degree is usually the first time a practitioner, educator or teacher engages in work-based research enquiry, and so becomes a researcher. This journey through the research process brings with it individual research stories, and develops the professional self, the self-image and self-esteem as contextually situated in the workplace (Miller and Cable, 2011). The development of the *learning professional* underpins professionalism and professional identity (Guille and Lucas, 1999) through a positive approach to continuing learning and development, in which the practitioner, educator or teacher seeks out opportunities to extend professional understandings and skill sets through study and research enquiry. Research on graduate experiences of an early years sector-endorsed foundation degree found personal and professional confidence to be raised through higher educational study that includes reflective work-based research (Hallet, 2009). In the following story of practice, a foundation degree graduate reflects on her professional development through her studies and research enquiry.

Story of practice: my research story

At the beginning of my job as a children's centre co-ordinator, I was seriously blagging it. I thought people would find me out; I'm a nursery nurse and I'd say to someone, 'oh, I've just said such and such!' But now I can do it, I've specialized knowledge about the early years as I've studied and researched it. I will talk to anyone and give presentations to large groups and answer any question.

An engagement in research and the beginning of an individual's research story will have a starting point, based on professional curiosity, a topic of interest, an observation of practice or policy. The purpose of research enquiry poses a question; it is wanting to find out more:

- How do children use talk in their learning?
- What is the importance of outdoor play in early learning?
- How do children feel about intervention programmes?
- What impact does classroom display have on teaching and learning?
- What are the expectations of male teachers in primary schools?
- How has continuing professional development impacted on practitioners' professionalism?

A research enquiry aims to make sense of practice or policy, listen to children's voices, understand ourselves as professionals, or develop new knowledge, understandings

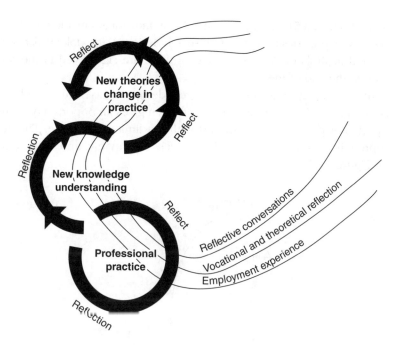

Figure 11.1 Spiral of reflective enquiry

and theories for change or modification of practice, as illustrated as a spiral of reflective enquiry in Figure 11.1.

This spiral of reflective enquiry as ongoing reflection throughout the research process is an agent for change in a practitioner, educator or teacher's thinking, in order to inform theory and influence an individual's practice. Three reflective threads link through the spiral of reflection: (1) employment experience; (2) vocational and theoretical reflection; and (3) reflective conversations with others, forming a model of work-based reflective learning (Hallet, 2013: 46) to enquire, research and improve practice.

Research enquiry

Personal and professionally held principles, values and beliefs, philosophies and ideologies underpin research enquiry (Clough and Nutbrown, 2007). These inform the methodological approach and paradigm underpinning the research, which are used to understand the research topic, structure the research, analyse the data and bring something to the knowledge, theory or practice constructed – this may be, for example, a child-centred, a feminist or an anti-discriminatory methodology (Mukherji and Albon, 2015; Roberts-Holmes, 2014). Selecting methods for collecting data, such as using questionnaires, conducting interviews, using the mosaic approach to listen to young children's views (Clark, 2005), may be informed by an individual's methodology. There are several step-by-step guides to help with research design, methodology, data collection methods and analysis of data, and some of these are signposted in the further reading section at the end of the chapter.

There are two main approaches to research design – case study and action research (Jarvis et al., 2012). The case study approach gives an opportunity to investigate an aspect of a problem in depth and within a limited timescale. The action research approach is a reflective, cyclic process of review and intervention, illustrated in Figure 11.2.

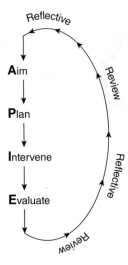

Figure 11.2   An action research cycle (A PIE)

Action research involves identifying an aspect of practice to investigate, change and improve through an intervention, evaluating its effects and then making a further change, evaluating again, and going round the cycle as many times as seems necessary (Jarvis et al., 2012). Figure 11.2 illustrates this in a metaphor of an early years pie (A PIE): aim, plan, intervene, evaluate … after a reflective review of the effectiveness of the intervention delivered, the cycle of a revised aim, planning, intervention and evaluation is repeated. In McNiff's (2014) view, action research and early years practice go together, as action research mirrors the entire process of children and teachers enjoying new experiences of learning together, and using their learning to create new futures. The following story of practice is a small-scale piece of action research demonstrating joint learning.

Story of practice: action research

Tana is studying on a foundation degree; she is a learning mentor in a primary school and talks about her research project, which involves investigating Year 1 boys' (aged 5 years) mark making in their early writing development.

My research was action research. I noticed over the space of a week, when I passed the mark-making table, there were only girls writing there. When the boys had free choice in play activity, they chose to build with construction toys, rather than mark-make at the writing table. I read up about boys' early writing and found that boys were generally less likely than girls to mark-make and write in their early years.

I thought, what could I do to encourage boys to make marks and develop those essential early writing skills? When the boys played, they tended to play in lots of space, using large movements and gross motor skills, rather than the fine motor skills that writing encouraged. As part of my action research, I introduced an intervention: play activities to encourage mark making. By putting large pieces of paper on the classroom floor with a box of felt-tipped pens, the boys started to scribble and mark-make, covering the large sheet of paper. By putting long strips of wallpaper in the playground outside with trays of paint, large paintbrushes and rollers, the boys started to mark-make in large circles, swirls, spirals, horizontal and vertical lines, making alphabetical and numerical shapes, using their gross motor skills in early mark making. With a bucket of water and large paintbrushes, the boys made marks on the playground and wrote on the classroom wall. This water writing seemed like magic to the boys, visible for a while, then disappearing in the sunshine. The boys particularly liked the outside activity as to them it was playing with paint and water, rather than mark making in early writing.

My action research project had successful intervention for practice, showing me the importance of providing learning experiences to suit differing learning styles, which may be different for boys and girls. To develop my research and interest in boys' writing, through the next cycle of action research I am going to come up with an outdoor play intervention to encourage the boys to write with purpose. My thinking has been influenced by the work of Nigel Hall (1999) who set out a garage in the nursery playground; he gave boys clipboards and pencils to write with, and they wrote down information and produced bills. I'm not sure exactly what I am going to do yet, as I've some more reading to do, but boys and their early writing is an interesting area and I want to find out more.

Learning through work-based research enquiry

Reflective learning is embedded within work-based research enquiry (Hallet, 2013). The workplace is a valid learning space where activities and interactions between the activity of work and those who work there take place (Allix, 2011). Work-based learning and practitioner research enquiry is a powerful pedagogy for professional learning and development (FDF, 2005). In Wenger's (1998) view, learning is an organic activity belonging to the realm of experience and practice. The work context transforms learning in a creative process (Hager, 2011), and knowledge is often created in action rather than before action (Marsick and Watkins, 1999), as the following story of practice shows (Hallet, 2013: 45).

Story of practice: reflecting on theory and practice

Sue is a manager of a private day nursery and a foundation degree graduate. Here, she reflects on her learning within her work-based practice.
    I started with *my practice* and then got to the *theory*. It's a cycle, how theory fits into practice and how to modify it. I read the theory to understand what I do.

The notion of linking theory with practice is important in research enquiry and developing early years practice. Having a sound knowledge of the research topic through an extensive review of relevant literature enables the researcher to connect their analysis of data and key findings to theory with practice or to practice with theory.

 ### Questions for reflection: linking practice with theory

As a practitioner, educator, teacher or student, identify an aspect of practice you have investigated, researched and found out about. This may be in relation to an assignment or an aspect of your work with children and families:

- How did you become interested in the topic?
- How did you learn more about the topic?
- How did you investigate or research the topic?
- How did you link theory with practice or practice with theory?
- Identify at least one key point you learned through your investigation or research enquiry.
- How has the knowledge gained influenced your practice?

Sharing and disseminating research

A key factor in the research process is sharing and disseminating research: how will others know about what you have found out? The purpose of research enquiry is to contribute to knowledge in the field of early childhood, to influence, change or modify provision, pedagogy, policy and practice. Sharing and disseminating research is an aspect of the research process that students undertaking research projects often miss out or add on at the end of writing up their research, but dissemination is central to the purpose of research enquiry. How can the key findings and messages be brought to the attention of the relevant decision makers, leaders, other practitioners, educators, teachers, parents and children? How can the key research findings influence expert conversation (Ruxton, 2014) and become transformative dialogue? (Pascal and Bertram, 2014).

To have an impact on policy and practice, researchers must do more than disseminate their evidence; it must be transformed and communicated to the right people (Kanefsky, 2001). The first step is to identify the relevant specialist and non-specialist audiences and stakeholders, and then to identify the most appropriate way to share the research through written or spoken language: a final report, an executive summary, a paper in an academic journal, an article in a professional magazine, via social media, blogs, the internet, being interviewed or taking part in a phone-in on local radio, contributing to a local or national newspaper. Media exposure can create the chance to communicate with non-specialists and shape popular thinking, particularly if the topic is current and newsworthy (Robb, 2014).

Presenting at staff meetings, local network groups, conferences or seminars is a way of communicating new research, offering an opportunity for researchers to present their findings and receive feedback. Conferences enable researchers to make connections with others doing similar work in the field, and to therefore place their research in the context of the wider conversation within their field of interest (Robb, 2014). These conversations can further shape the research enquiry.

Impact of research on policy and practice

Practice-led research is now accepted as making an important contribution to the knowledge base of early childhood (Pascal and Bertram, 2014). There is an increasing focus on the way knowledge developed from research becomes embedded within organizations, interwoven with their priorities, cultures and contexts (Nutley et al., 2010). The New Labour government in England promoted the concept of 'evidence-based policy' and the notion that decision makers should pay attention to the evidence produced by researchers to impact on improvements in policy development and positive outcomes in practice. As research is contested, the lesser term 'evidence-informed policy' is preferred (Ruxton, 2014: 266). Evidence from government-funded research studies (Brooker et al., 2010; Nutbrown, 2012; Tickell, 2011) has informed a recent government review of early years education and the development of early years policy in England.

The EPPE 3–11 study, funded by the Department for Education and Skills, is an example of a high-profile study that provided evidence to inform early years policy development (Taggart et al., 2008). Through a knowledge exchange partnership between researchers and policy makers working together in shaping, implementing and disseminating their research, knowledge is jointly created and evaluated (Sylva et al., 2007). Effective knowledge exchange involves interaction between decision makers and researchers, resulting in mutual learning through the process of planning, producing, disseminating and applying existing or new research in decision making. It is argued that the 'knowledge exchange partnership' facilitated the direct use of EPPE findings in formulating policy (Sylva et al., 2007: 161). This is demonstrated in recent government policy; universal pre-school provision, targeted services and integrated practice in disadvantaged communities, as in Sure Start children's centres; the use of sustained shared thinking in the EYFS; and the introduction of a higher qualified workforce and the development of graduate early years teachers. Similarly, a key finding in the Department for Education's funded research, *Practitioners' experiences of the Early Years Foundation Stage* (Brooker et al., 2010), identified the over-assessment of Early Learning Goals (ELG) as burdensome for teachers. This informed the Tickell Review of EYFS (2011) and the subsequent reduction of ELGs in the revised EYFS (DfE, 2014a).

For research to change practice, it must be immersed in practice. Pascal and Bertram (2014) use a participatory paradigm and participatory research methods as a means to change practice with praxis (reflection and action) carried out with others as transformative agency. Through democratic participation, research participants, who may be adults or children, are empowered to generate knowledge that generates change (Pascal and Bertram, 2014). Practitioners, educators and teachers value research when it is focused on specific teaching and learning contexts (Galton, 2000). When a professional learning culture has been developed in a school that encourages reflective continuing professional development then changes in practice emerge (Earley and Porritt, 2009). Galton (2000) argues that few educational research interventions have led to sustained change. However, sustained change over time demonstrates the long-term impact of research on policy and practice.

Autobiographical reflective enquiry

Before autobiographical reflective enquiry is considered, it must be contextually situated within the concept of professionalism in the early years sector, which emerged due to workforce reform (Miller and Cable, 2008). Professionalism is a discourse as much as a phenomenon, constantly under construction within national and international frameworks, and conceptually complex, given a cluster of related concepts – being professional, behaving professionally, working with professional autonomy and having a professional identity (Dalli and Urban, 2008). In New Zealand, an aspect of professionalism is regarded as professional knowledge-in-the-making (Duhn, 2011) and the learning self (Guille and Lucas, 1999) is seen as the basis for professionalism, with an engagement with people, things, ideas, policies and politics as part of an ongoing discourse. Democratic professionalism (Moss, 2008) includes the skills needed for research enquiry, such as participatory relationships, listening, being open to other views, reflective dialogue with others, critical thinking, questioning, research and enquiry, multiple perspectives and curiosity, and developing a knowledge base. Researching early years practice builds a knowledge base for policy and practice, which is an important aspect of professionalism and being professional.

Autobiographical self-reflection is one of the most important forms of narrative for developing skills of critique and enquiry around one's professional practice (Bold, 2012). Practitioners, educators and teachers have personal and professional life histories – by reflecting on their individual life history, they are able to make sense of their influences, values, beliefs, constructs and pedagogy for working with children and families. These 'lived experiences' and 'lived relationships' are personal and professional journeys of enquiry, learning and discovery (Clough and Corbett, 2000: 156). Personal and professional aspects of practitioners' life histories are intertwined, giving each other significance and contributing to the development of professional identity (Court et al., 2009). Life histories link analytical and reflective thinking to an individual's experience of practice. Learning is developed through experience and enquiry, and reflective learning and enquiry inform reflective practice (Paige-Smith and Craft, 2011). Appleby (2010: 9) describes reflective practice as a never-ending learning journey, as stories of experience and enquiry (Bolton, 2014) that develop professional understanding. There is opportunity for you to reflect on your story of experience and understand your professional self in the following questions for reflection.

Questions for reflection: Who am I?
My professional self

- Draw a picture of your 'work self' – your professional self in your work setting or work placement. Represent your professional self with illustrations and words.
- Choose an object from your work setting or work placement to represent some, or all, principles, values and beliefs of your pedagogy and practice. Write some notes to share with others.

(Continued)

(Continued)

The aim of these activities is to enquire about influences on your professional self and your professional identity:

- In small groups, with a friend or colleague, use your drawing and object to share your professional self and professional identity with others, answering any questions to further understanding.

There are many aspects to professional practice when working with children. The seven words in the list below describe aspects of a practitioner's role in enabling children's learning and development. They provide a focus for enquiring about your practice with children and families (Hallet, 2008: 78, adapted).

 Questions for reflection: enquiring about my practice

For each aspect listed below, give an example from your practice or work placement experience:

- *Supplying* – providing opportunities
- *Supporting* – valuing, intervening, extending
- *Scaffolding* – helping confidence and independence
- *Sharing* – talking, listening, asking questions, sustained shared thinking
- *Showing* – demonstrating, being a role model
- *Saying* – praising, encouraging, giving constructive feedback
- *Seeing* – observing and planning for future learning

On completion, share with someone who has a different role to you:

- Are there any similarities or differences in your roles and practices?
- What have you learnt about your practice?
- What are the strengths of your practice?
- What aspect of your practice can you develop?

Implications for practice

We are born as action researchers, as people who wish to find ways of improving our learning, and using that learning to improve our practices in the world.

McNiff's (2014: xi) view encapsulates the purpose of being a researcher and researching early years practice. The notion that those who work with children are action researchers has implications for practice. For research to affect practice or policy, an organization needs to have a research culture at its centre and a key driver in the development of policy and practice, time given to those who work there to carry out research, and importantly time to share and disseminate research within the organization and to the wider early childhood field.

 Further reading

Level 4

Mukherji, P. and Albon, D. (2015) *Research methods in early childhood: an introductory guide* (2nd edn). London: Sage.
This book guides the reader in doing research on early childhood, and the companion website gives helpful information on doing research.

Level 5

Walker, R. and Solvason, C. (2014) *Success with your early years research project.* London: Sage.
The examples of students' action research projects in this book, with commentaries from the authors, guide the development of a good research project.

Level 6

The European Early Childhood Education Research Journal
The Journal of Early Childhood Research
These two journals disseminate a wide range of national and international research studies.

NCTL Teachers' Standards (Early Years)

Standard 4.5
- Reflect on and evaluate teaching activities and educational programmes to support the continuous improvement of provision.

Roberts-Holmes, G. (2014) *Doing your early years research project: a step-by-step guide* (3rd edn). London: Sage.
This book scaffolds the reader through the practical elements of designing, implementing and evaluating their research project.

Chapter 12

Leading Early Years Practice

Chapter overview

This chapter explores the phenomenon of early years leadership within the current context of professional leadership development. Government policy concerning the development of a workforce of graduate leaders through higher educational professional awards and the development of leadership roles is examined. Research studies on early years leadership are referred to within the discussion. The following aspects of leadership are considered: inclusive leadership, influencing leadership and gender within leadership. A model of early years leadership developed from research is explored to consider leadership style and practice. There is opportunity to reflect on early years leadership practice.

Leadership within the early years context

The development of professionalism and the raising of the status of the early years workforce are linked with leadership in national and international ECEC contexts (Dalli and Urban, 2008). Professionalism and leadership in the early years are complex phenomena – 'like a ball of knotted string' (Friedman, 2007: 126), the ball is beginning to unravel and reveal understandings about professional leadership of practice within the context of early years care and education. Research studies on early years leadership that have contributed to understanding include: Effective Leadership and Management in the Early Years (ELMS-EY) (Moyles, 2006); Effective Leadership in the Early Years Sector (the ELEYS study) (Siraj-Blatchford and Manni, 2007); and the Longitudinal Study of Graduate Leader Training (EYPS) (Hadfield et al., 2011). These studies illuminate the phenomenon of leadership in the early years, providing insights into leadership and management roles and responsibilities.

The ELEYS study (Siraj-Blatchford and Manni, 2007: 28) researched the leadership of learning within the early years sector, identifying requirements for the leadership of learning as *contextual literacy*, a commitment to *collaboration* and the *improvement* of children's learning outcomes. The ELEYS study identified 10 effective leadership practices in effective pre-school settings:

1. *Identifying and articulating a collective vision*, especially with regard to pedagogy and curriculum.
2. *Ensuring shared understandings*: building common purposes.
3. *Using effective communication*: providing a level of transparency in regard to expectations, practices and processes.
4. *Encouraging reflection*: which acts as an impetus for change and a motivation for ongoing learning and development.
5. *Monitoring and assessing practice*: through collaborative dialogue and action research.
6. *Showing commitment to ongoing professional development*: supporting staff to become more critically reflective in their practice.
7. *Encouraging distributed leadership*: involving staff in the leadership of their setting.
8. *Building a learning community and a team culture*: establishing a community of learners.
9. *Encouraging and facilitating parent and community partnerships*: promoting achievement for all young children by working with parents and carers.
10. *Leading and managing – striking a balance*: balancing administrative managerial tasks with teaching and learning.

In the research study *Leadership of learning in early years practice* (the LLEaP project) (Hallet, 2014), investigating early years professionals' (EYPs) leadership practice, the ELEYS study's characteristics of effective leadership practice, listed above, were used as a framework for analysis, identifying early years leaders' best leadership practice in six pre-school settings as shown in Figure 12.1.

Questions for reflection: effective leadership practice

- Using the ELEYS study's list of effective leadership practices as a checklist, observe these leadership practices in your work setting or placement. Write a comment about the evidence you have observed or not observed, in relation to each characteristic of effective early years leadership.
- When your observation is complete, write a narrative reflecting on the evidence for effective leadership practice you have collected. Consider areas of strength and areas for development.

Leading and managing

'Leadership and management' are terms used frequently within the early years sector, the two concepts being tied together and interchangeably used. The two should be separated, as leadership and management have differing characteristics, roles and responsibilities that can cause tensions and challenges in organizations, if not fully understood (Whalley, 2011). The ELEYS study highlights differences in leading and managing, with the ability of effective early years leaders 'to strike a balance' between administrative tasks and tasks associated with teaching and learning being important. The differing roles can cause tension – 'the difficulty of balancing these seemingly disparate tasks has often seen one, the administrative role, taking precedence over the other, leading teaching and learning' (Siraj-Blatchford and Manni, 2007: 25). Whalley (2011) defines roles and responsibilities for leaders and managers: a manager has a planning and organizational role, coordinates the organization, clarifies work roles, makes decisions for the daily running of the organization and generally monitors for effectiveness. A leader's role is to provide a vision that is shared by others, give direction, offer inspiration, build teamwork, influence others and be a demonstrator of effective leadership and professional practice. The role of EYPs as leaders of practice has aided the understanding of differences in leaders' and managers' roles and responsibilities within a setting.

Inclusive early years leadership

The importance of a well-qualified workforce and the contribution of graduate leadership in the early years sector is acknowledged in the Tickell Review of the

EYFS curriculum (Tickell, 2011) and the Nutbrown Review of Early Education and Childcare Qualifications (Nutbrown, 2012). These reviews highlighted the value of pedagogical leadership of practice and particularly the role of teachers in supporting educational outcomes for children. Nutbrown (2012: 55) identifies the need for career progression in the early years workforce and for the sector to raise the aspirations of those who work with babies and young children: 'ultimately, all early years leaders should aspire to be leaders, of practice, if not of settings, and all practitioners should be capable of demonstrating pedagogical leadership regardless of qualification level'. The inclusive nature of early years leadership is that it is accessible to all staff members, irrespective of their qualifications. These differing levels of leadership include: leading practice within a room, leading practice across a number of rooms, leading practice across a setting, and providing overall leadership for a setting. Inclusive leadership moves away from the traditional understanding of hierarchical leadership being associated with a single person with the authority to lead, undertake and carry out tasks alone (Rodd, 2013). Leadership in the early years is being conceptually revised, with inclusive and shared leadership emerging from within a setting, school or children's centre, with educators, teachers and practitioners having the opportunity to lead on aspects of provision and practice (McDowall Clark and Murray, 2012). Sharing leadership empowers others and develops leadership capacity and capability within a setting, school or children's centre (Siraj and Hallet, 2014).

Leadership in early childhood appears to be more about the result of groups of people who work together to influence and inspire, rather than the efforts of one single person who focuses on getting the job done (Rodd, 2013). As changes in schools, settings and children's centres are introduced, due to government review of provision, those working in the early years have leadership roles and responsibilities and work within a 'leaderful community' of shared or distributed leadership (Raelin, 2003: 44). The collective team can undertake differing leadership roles, actions and functions under the deliberate action of a designated leader who delegates leadership tasks and responsibilities (Jones and Pound, 2008). This is particularly evident in leading integrated practice in which health, education and social services professionals work together in a multi-agency team. The emerging range of leadership roles, such as family support team leader, intervention coordinator, parent advisory team leader, extended schools service coordinator, requires a change in how leadership is viewed in early years settings, children's centres and schools (Duffy and Marshall, 2007) – from a single leader to the leadership of specialist teams. Effective team leadership, in which leadership is distributed and shared, results in high-quality interaction between team members, a culture of trust and openness, and shared understandings (Rodd, 2013).

Influencing leadership

Whalley (1999) suggests that women prefer an influencing style of leadership, rather than an authoritarian style in undertaking a leadership role. An empowering, collaborative style of leadership, developed through relational culture, is associated with women rather than the authoritarian style of men; this leadership style tends to be more democratic and participatory, encouraging inclusiveness (Collard and Reynolds, 2005). An influencing leadership style is based on relationships; through interpersonal and communication skills, active listening and negotiation, women are able to lead and empower others through demonstration and influence. In the ELEYS study, Siraj-Blatchford and Manni (2007) found that effective leaders are those who influence and develop others by example. In the following story of practice, an early years leader in the LLEaP project talks about her influencing style of leadership practice (Hallet, 2014).

Story of practice: influencing others

Alison is the playgroup leader of a community playgroup. She has six play leaders in her team; here, she reflects on her leadership style and ways of influencing her staff.

I don't see myself as a leader but like 'an ant', scurrying about trying to encourage best practice by sharing my knowledge. I've benefitted from higher education but not everyone can afford this, so I share my knowledge with staff. I might bring in an article from a professional magazine like *The Early Years Educator* and say, 'have you seen this?' Or 'shall we try this activity?' I demonstrate practice by working alongside staff at an activity with children. I'm committed to raising the quality of provision and try to influence others by my enthusiasm, specialized knowledge and practice.

 Questions for reflection: influencing others

- Choose an example, from your professional practice or personal life, of a situation where you have influenced others.
- How did you lead by influencing others in this example?
- How do you know your influencing leadership was effective?

Gender within early years leadership

The demographics of the early years workforce in England show that it is predominantly women who work with young children and families (Nutbrown, 2012; Siraj-Blatchford and Manni, 2007). In European countries like Denmark and Norway, more men work with young children (Peeters, 2007). Internationally, the only area of education where most leaders are women is in early years provision (Lumby and Coleman, 2007). Historically, the care of young children is traditionally associated with the caring, nurturing attributes of mothering (Osgood, 2012). Women working in ECEC invest heavily in a 'mother-like identity', promoting a nurturing, caring feminized culture, which can challenge the integration of male workers within the early years workforce (Ailwood, 2007). However, there is a tendency for men working in female-dominated areas to gain promotion and become leaders (Lumby and Coleman, 2007). In Rodd's (2013) view, there is reluctance in some women practitioners, educators and teachers to identify aspects of leadership in their work role and to aspire to leadership as a career objective.

Ethics of care within the early years sector (Osgood, 2006) have perhaps influenced the perceptions of those undertaking the leadership roles they often find themselves in and their reluctance to identify themselves as leaders (Rodd, 2013). There has been a general hesitance in early years leaders working in an educational school context to recognize leadership as part of their professional role, valuing more their teaching work (Kagan and Hallmark, 2001). The gendered nature of women's leadership style has an element of care in its nurturing and collaborative practices. As demonstrated in Figure 12.1, a model of early years leadership developed from the LLEaP project on graduate leadership in private, voluntary and independent (PVI) settings in one local authority. The research participants were all women leaders (Hallet and Roberts-Holmes, 2010).

This model of early years leadership illustrates the relational leadership style within the PVI early years sector. Those early years leaders who were early years professionals (EYPs) in the LLEaP project demonstrated an early years leadership style that is holistic, nurturing, caring, inclusive, democratic and collaborative, encompassing the children, parents, community and staff the setting serves, a leadership style underpinned by experience of working in early years practice with children and families. The leadership style in the LLEaP project was collaborative, with decisions being taken democratically. The settings in the research study (playgroups, pre-schools, daycare) were small in size and without the linear leadership and management hierarchy found in schools, enabling a diffused level of accountability and parity in decision-making processes. Decisions were made through existing collaborative team cultures in the settings that the leaders had established by developing partnerships amongst members of staff through trust and respect, as found in the ELEYS study (Siraj-Blatchford and Manni, 2007).

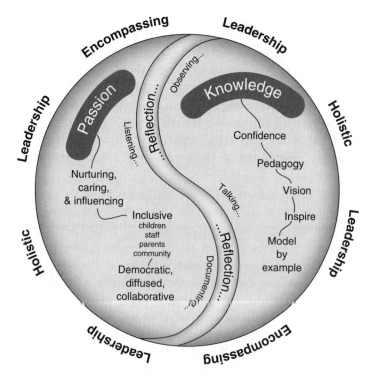

Figure 12.1 Model of early years leadership

The women's leadership style in the LLEaP project has three drivers: *passion* and *specialized knowledge* informed by a thread of *reflection*. Passion gives emotional agency for those working in the early years sector, particularly women leaders. An emotional enthusiasm, a deep and sound commitment, often described as a passion or being passionate, is often expressed by those working with young children, as it brings them close to children, families and communities (Moyles, 2001). Successful leaders are those who have a 'deep-seated passion' for children, and for the setting and community in which they work (Moyles, 2006: 9), and a 'natural enthusiasm for children, teaching and learning is a personal characteristic and attribute of an early years leader' (Moyles, 2006: 14). Enthusiasm, passion, inspiration and advocacy are valuable strengths for leadership (Solley, 2003); as Goleman (2002) highlights, strong leaders are emotionally intelligent and inspire, arouse passion and enthusiasm, keeping staff motivated and committed.

The early years leaders in the LLEaP project emerged as a group with specialist knowledge and understanding underpinned by experience of working in early years provision and practice. The specialized knowledge gained in higher education gave them the professional confidence to articulate their knowledge and lead pedagogy for teaching and learning, provision and practice. Their specialized knowledge enables them to develop a vision shared by staff, parents and carers. A vision is often the driving force in influencing others and leading change. Visionary leaders have a view for the future informed by principles and values cognate to the early years phase of learning and development (Jones and Pound, 2008). The ELEYS study showed that in the most effective settings, leadership was characterized by a clear vision with regard to pedagogy and curriculum that was shared by all those working in the setting (Siraj-Blatchford and Manni, 2007). Identifying and articulating a collective vision is one of the defining characteristics of effective leadership identified in the ELEYS study.

Reflection

A thread of reflection informed the style of early years leadership in Figure 12.1. The early years leaders in the LLEaP project were reflective leaders; through observation, documenting, active listening and talking, they continually reflected on their leadership style and practice. Leaders have a responsibility for self-development and to develop their pedagogy for leadership, to develop and support others as leaders and to lead change within an organization (Siraj-Blatchford and Hallet, 2012). Reflection provides agency for this process. Effective leaders are reflective in their own practice and encourage reflection in their staff (Siraj-Blatchford and Manni, 2007). They engage with others in reflective dialogue to change and modify practice, leading by example, modelling practice and influencing others. A setting, school or children's centre with collaborative, reflective processes at its heart is evolving and changing (Hallet, 2013). The challenge is to find time and space for reflection, which is not always easy in a busy setting, school or children's centre. Recording children's educational progress through documenting learning is used for reflective dialogue between teachers, parents and children. This reflective discussion makes visible the learning processes and strategies used by each child (Rinaldi, 2005).

Graduate early years leadership

Evidence from research identifies the importance of graduate leaders; particularly teachers and those who supervised others have contributed significantly to pedagogy, provision and practice for pre-school children (the EPPE study). The introduction of EYPs who were graduate early years leaders of practice, whose role was to lead practice across the EYFS, support and mentor others (Whalley, 2011), raised the importance of leadership within early years education and recognized the contribution of highly qualified leaders to children's learning and development.

In the last 15 years, developing a more highly qualified early years workforce in England has been addressed through nationally recognized professional awards at graduate-degree level. The Sector-Endorsed Early Years Foundation Degree (EYSEFD) developed the role of Senior Practitioner. Early Years Professional Status (EYPS) developed the role of the Early Years Professional as a leader of practice. The National Professional Qualification in Integrated Centre Leadership (NPQICL) for Sure Start children's centre leaders provided nationally recognized standards for leadership training and defined leadership standards for integrated practice (Siraj-Blatchford and Hallet, 2012). The current introduction of Teachers' Standards (Early Years) (NCTL, 2013), which operate in parallel with Teachers' Standards for the graduate award of qualified teacher status (QTS), develops the role of an Early Years Teacher (EYT), a pedagogical leader, leading pedagogy and practice for children from birth to 5 years of age.

These programmes, publically funded, widen access to higher education for many early years practitioners, particularly women (Hallet, 2013). Such professional awards raise the level of qualifications to graduate level and to the professional status, and the personal and professional confidence of the early years workforce (Hadfield et al., 2011). A workforce with specialist early years knowledge has emerged. The longitudinal study of graduate-level professional development (EYPS) demonstrated the significant contribution of higher educational learning on the skills, status and confidence of practitioners and the positive impact of graduate-led leadership in affecting change and improving early years provision (Hadfield et al., 2011). Similarly, foundation-degree graduates of an EYSEFD develop professional knowledge and confidence (Hallet, 2013). The 'invisible workforce' of nursery nurses 'quietly washing the paint pots in the corner of the classroom' has emerged, through higher educational professional learning, into a 'visible workforce' with knowledge and agency, with a professional identity, in the forefront of leading government policy into practice (Hallet, 2013: 1).

Implications for practice

Our youngest children deserve the best leaders to prepare them for the challenges they will face as they move forward into adulthood.

Nelson's view (2011: xi) highlights the importance of effective leaders for young children's learning and development. Evidence from research supports this view: there was a higher quality of provision that integrated care and education and was led by a qualified teacher who supervised less qualified staff (Sylva et al., 2004). In setting out a vision for early education and childcare, the Truss report

(Continued)

(Continued)

(Truss, 2013) places importance on high-quality early education and childcare, delivered with love and care, as having a powerful impact on young children. Therefore, the qualifications of staff are significant to the quality of provision, resonated in the graduate training of early years teachers (EYTs) as pedagogical leaders of practice. A developing awareness of the impact of early years leadership on the quality of provision has implications for practice. Therefore, the use of inclusive leadership provides an opportunity for practitioners, educators and teachers to lead early years practice, building a workforce of experienced leaders. The developing role of early years teachers as leaders of pedagogy and practice contributes to the agenda for high-quality provision and improved educational outcomes for young children.

 Further reading

Level 4

Siraj-Blatchford, I. and Manni, L. (2007) *Effective leadership in the early years sector (ELEYS study)*. London: Institute of Education.
This book disseminates this research study about early years leadership.

Level 5

Rodd, J. (2013) *Leadership in early childhood: the pathway to professionalism* (3rd edn). Maidenhead: Open University Press.
This book discusses the challenges and approaches to leadership in early childhood contexts.

Level 6

Siraj, I. and Hallet, E. (2014) *Effective and caring leadership in the early years*. London: Sage.
This book discusses effective and caring leadership within a model of relational leadership that is firmly based in research and professional experience.

McDowall Clark, R. (2012) '"I've never thought of myself as a leader but…": early years professional and catalytic leadership', *European Early Childhood Education Research Journal*, 20 (3) 391–401.

The concept of catalytic leadership, whereby graduate early years leaders inspire change rather than lead change through power, is discussed in this journal article.

NCTL Teachers' Standards (Early Years)

Standard 8.4

• Model and implement effective education and care, and support and lead other practitioners including early years educators.

Hallet, E. (2014) *Leadership of learning in early years practice: a professional learning resource*. London: Institute of Education Press.

This book is developed from the LLEaP research study on early years leaders' practices referred to in this chapter. The book comprehensively examines the complexity of early years leadership with a particular focus on the leadership of learning in early years practice. The examples of leadership practice in the accompanying DVD offer excellent insight into aspects of early years leadership of learning and encourage readers to reflect critically on approaches to leadership practice in early years settings.

Matrix

Inclusion of NCTL Teachers' Standards (Early Years) in Chapter Content

Group of Standards	Chapters											
	1	2	3	4	5	6	7	8	9	10	11	12
Standards 1 Group Set high expectations which inspire, motivate and challenge all children				x	x	x	x	x		x		
Standards 2 Group Promote good progress and outcomes by children				x		x			x	x		
Standards 3 Group Demonstrate good knowledge of early learning and EYFS				x		x	x	x				
Standards 4 Group Plan education and care, taking account of the needs of all children	x	x		x	x				x	x	x	
Standards 5 Group Adapt education and care to respond to the strengths and needs of all children				x					x	x		
Standards 6 Group Make accurate and productive use of assessment		x										
Standards 7 Group Safeguard and promote the welfare of children and provide a safe learning environment		x										
Standards 8 Group Fulfill wider professional responsibilities	x		x							x	x	x

Glossary of Terms

B-3	Birth to 3 matters framework
C4EO	Centre for Excellence and Outcomes
CAF	Common assessment framework
CPD	Continuing professional development
CWDC	Children's Workforce Development Council
DAP	Developmentally appropriate curriculum
DfE	Department for Education
DfES	Department for Education and Skills
ECE	Early childhood education
ECEC	Early childhood education and care
ECERS-E	Early Childhood Environmental Rating Scale – Extension
ECM	Every child matters
ELEYS	Effective Leadership in the Early Years Sector (ELEYS study)

EPPE	Effective Provision of Pre-school Education (EPPE) project
EPPE	3–11 Effective Pre-school and Primary Education (3–11) project
EPPSE	Effective Pre-school, Primary and Secondary Education (3–16) study
EYFS	Early years foundation stage
EYFSP	Early years foundation stage profile
EYP	Early years professional
EYPS	Early years professional status
EYSEFD	Early years sector-endorsed foundation degree
EYTS	Early years teacher status
FS	Foundation stage curriculum (Northern Ireland)
GCSE	General Certificate of Secondary Education
HLE	Home learning environment
HLTA	Higher level teaching assistant
LLEaP	Leadership of Learning in Early Years Practice (the LLEaP project)
NPQICL	National Professional Qualification for Integrated Centre Leaders
OECD	Organisation for Economic Co-operation and Development
ORIM	The ORIM framework
QTS	Qualified teacher status
REPEY	Researching Effective Pedagogy in the Early Years (REPEY) study
SEN	Special educational needs
SENCO	Special educational needs co-ordinator
SST	Sustained shared thinking
SSTEW	Sustained Shared Thinking and Emotional Well-being (SSTEW) scale
TA	Teaching assistant
UNCRC	United Nations Convention on the Rights of the Child
ZPD	Zone of proximal development

References

Abbas, T. (2007) 'British South Asians and pathways into selective schooling: social class, culture and ethnicity', *British Educational Research Journal*, 33 (1) 75–91.

Abbott, L. and Nutbrown, C. (eds) (2001) *Experiencing Reggio Emilia*. Maidenhead: Open University Press.

Adams, K. (2008) 'What's in a name? Seeking professional status through degree studies within the Scottish early years context', Special Issue, *Professionalism in Early Childhood Education and Care: European Early Childhood Education Research Journal*, 16 (2) 242–54.

Aguirre Jones, D. and Elders, L. (2009) '5x5x5=creativity in practice', in S. Bancroft, M. Fawcett and P. Hay (eds) *Researching children researching the world: 5x5x5= creativity*. Stoke-on-Trent: Trentham Books.

Ailwood, S. (2007) 'Mothers, teachers, maternalism and early childhood education and care: some historical connections', *Contemporary Issues in Early Childhood*, 8 (2) 157–65.

Ainscow, M. (1999) *Understanding the development of inclusive schools*. London: Falmer Press.

Alexander, R. (ed.) (2010) *Children, their world, their education: Final report and recommendations of the Cambridge Review of Primary Education*. Abingdon: Routledge.

Allen, G. (2011) *Early intervention: the next steps*. London: Her Majesty's Government.

Allix, N. (2011) 'Knowledge and workplace learning', in M. Malloch, L. Cairns, K. Evans and B.N. O'Conner (eds) *The international handbook of workplace learning: theory, research, practice and issues*. London: Sage.

Ang, L. (ed.) (2014) *The early years curriculum: the UK context and beyond*. Abingdon: Routledge.

Anning, A. and Edwards, A. (2010) 'Young children as learners', in L. Miller, C. Cable and G. Goodliff (eds) *Supporting Children's Learning in the Early Years* (2nd edn). Maidenhead: Open University Press.

Appleby, K. (2010) 'Reflective thinking: reflective practice', in M. Reed and N. Canning (eds) *Reflective Practice in the Early Years*. London: Sage.

Atherton, F. and Nutbrown, C. (2013) *Understanding schema and young children*. London: Sage.

Australian Government (2009) *The Early Years Learning Framework for Australia: Belonging, being and becoming*. Available at: www.coag.gov.au/sites/default/files/early_years_learning_framework.pdf

Balbernie, R. and Zeedyk, S. (2010) *Pre-birth to three: new national guidelines*. www.educationscotland.gov.uk (accessed 10.07.14).

Baldock, P., Fitzgerald, D. and Kay, J. (2013) *Understanding early years policy* (3rd edn). London: Sage.

Ball, C. (1994) *Start right report*. London: Royal Society of Arts.

Barnett, W.S. (2004) 'Better teachers, better preschools: student achievement linked to teacher qualifications', *Pre-school Policy Matters,* Issue 2. New Brunswick, NJ: NIEER.

Beals, D. (1998) 'Re-appropriating schema: conceptions of development from Barlett and Bathtin', *Mind, Culture and Activity*, 5 (1) 5–24.

Beauchamp, C. and Thomas, L. (2009) 'Understanding teacher identity: an overview of issues in literature and implications for teacher education', *Cambridge Journal of Education*. 39 (2): 175–89.

Beckley, P. (2012) 'Partnerships with parents/carers', in P. Beckley (ed.) *Learning in the early years*. London: Sage.

Bedford, D. and Wilson, E. (2013) *Study skills for foundation degrees* (2nd edn). London: Routledge.

Beeley, K. (2012) *Science in the early years: understanding the world through play-based learning*. London: Featherstone Education.

Beetlestone, F. (1998) *Creative children, imaginative teaching*. Maidenhead: Open University Press.

Blackwell, S. and Pound, L. (2011) 'Forest schools in the early years', in, L. Miller and L. Pound (eds) *Theories and approaches to learning in the early years*. London: Sage.

Bold, C. (2012) *Using narrative in research*. London: Sage.

Bolton, G. (2014) *Reflective practice: writing and professional development* (4th edn). London: Sage.

Booth, T., Ainscow, M. and Kingston, D. (2006) *Index for inclusion*. Bristol: Centre for Studies on Inclusive Education.

Bowlby, J. (1969) *Attachment and loss, Vol. 1: Attachment*. New York: Basic Books and Hogarth Press.

Broadhead, P., Howard, J. and Wood, E. (eds) (2010) *Play and learning in the early years*. London: Sage.

Brock, A. and Ranklin, C. (2008) *Communication, language and literacy from birth to five*. London: Sage.

Brockliss, L. and Montgomery, H. (2013) 'Childhood: a historical approach', in J. Kelly (ed.) (2013) *Understanding childhood: a cross-disciplinary approach*. Bristol: The Policy Press.

Bronfenbrenner, U. (1979) *The ecology of human development*. Cambridge, MA: Harvard University Press.

Brooker, E., Rogers, S., Ellis, D., Hallet, E. and Roberts-Holmes, G. (2010) *Practitioners' experiences of the early years foundation stage*. Ref. DfE-RR029. London: DfE.

Brooker, L. (2002) *Starting school: young children learning cultures*. Buckingham: Open University Press.

Brooker, L. (2008) *Supporting transitions in the early years*. Maidenhead: Open University Press.

Brooker, L. (2012) '"Just like having a best friend": how babies and toddlers construct relationships with their key workers in nurseries', in L. Miller, R. Drury and C. Cable (eds) *Extending professional practice in the early years*. Milton Keynes: Open University Press.

Brookfield, S. (1995) *Becoming a critically reflective teacher*. San Francisco: Jossey-Bass.

Browne, N. (2004) *Gender equity in the early years*. Maidenhead: Open University Press.

Bruce, T. (1987) *Early childhood education*. London: Hodder & Stoughton.

Bruce, T. (2001) *Learning through play*. London: Hodder & Stoughton.

Bruce, T. (2005) 'Play matters', in L. Abbott and A. Langston (eds) *Birth to three matters: supporting the framework of effective practice*. Maidenhead: Open University Press.

Bruce, T. and Spratt, J. (2008) *Essentials of literacy from 0–7*. London: Sage.

Bubb, S. and Earley, P. (2007) *Leading and managing continuing professional development* (2nd edn). London: Paul Chapman Publishing.

Carr, M. (2001) *Assessment in early childhood: learning stories.* London: Sage.

Carr, M. and Lee, W. (2012) *Learning stories: constructing learner identities in early education.* London: Sage.

Carruthers, E. and Worthington, M. (2011) *Understanding children's mathematical graphics.* Maidenhead: Open University Press.

Central Advisory Council for Education (CACE) (1967) *The Plowden Report: children and their primary school.* London: HMSO.

Centre for Excellence and Outcomes (C4EO) (2010) *Grasping the nettle: early intervention for children, families and communities.* London: C4EO.

Clark, A. (2005) *Beyond listening: children's perspectives on early childhood services.* London: Policy Press.

Clough, P. and Corbett, J. (2000) *Theories of inclusive education: a student's guide.* London: Paul Chapman/Sage.

Clough, P. and Nutbrown, C. (2007) *A student's guide to methodology* (2nd edn). London: Sage.

Collard, J. and Reynolds, C. (eds) (2005) *Leadership, gender and culture in education: male and female perspectives.* Maidenhead: Open University Press.

Collins, K. (2014) Tackling the attainment gap in the early years: how evidence can help. Education endowment foundation blog, 15 September. Available at: https://educationendowmentfoundation.org.uk/news/eef-blog-tackling-the-attainment-gap-in-the-early-years-how-evidence-can-he/

Constable, K. (2013) *Planning for schematic learning in the early years.* London: Routledge.

Corbett, J. and Slee, R. (2000) 'An international conversation on inclusive education', in F. Armstrong, D. Armstrong and L. Barton (eds) *Inclusive policy, contexts and comparative perspectives.* London: David Fulton.

Cortvriend, V. and MacLeod-Brudenell, I. (2004) Observation and Assessment, in I. MacLeod-Brudenell (ed.) (2004) *Advanced early years education and care for levels 4 and 5.* Oxford: Heinemann Educational.

Cottle, M. and Alexander, E. (2012) 'Quality in early years settings: government, research and practitioners' perspectives', *British Educational Research Journal*, 38 (4) 635–54.

Coughlan, S. (2008) 'Is five too soon to start school?', BBC News, 8 February. Available at: http://news.bbc.co.uk/1/hi/education/7234578.stm (accessed July 2014).

Council for the Curriculum, Examinations and Assessment (CCEA) (2014) Northern Ireland Curriculum. Available at: www.nicurriculum.org.uk/ (accessed December 2014).

Court, D., Merav, I. and Oren, E. (2009) 'Pre-school teachers' narratives: a window on personal professional history, values and beliefs', *International Journal of Early Years Education*, 17 (3) 207–17.

Cowdray, M. (2013) *Children's learning in the primary schools*. Abingdon: Routledge.

Cox, J. (2014) 'The Reggio Emilia approach to early childhood education', in L. Ang (ed.) *The early years curriculum: the UK context and beyond*. Abingdon: Routledge.

Craft, A. (2002*) Creativity and early years education*. London: Continuum.

Craft, A., Cremin, T. and Burnard, P. (eds) (2008) *Creative learning 3–11*. Stoke-on-Trent: Trentham Books.

Creative Little Scientists (CLS) (2015) *Creativity in science and mathematics education for young children: executive summary*. www.creative-little-scientists.eu (accessed January 2015).

Cressey, P. and Boud, D. (2006) 'The emergence of productive reflection', in D. Boud, P. Cressey and P. Docherty (eds) *Productive reflection at work*. London: Routledge.

Dalli, C. and Urban, M. (eds) (2008) 'Editorial', Special Issue, *Professionalism in Early Childhood Education and Care*, 16 (2) 3–13.

Department for Children, Schools and Families (DCSF) (2007) *The Children's Plan*. London: DCSF.

Department for Children, Schools and Families (DCSF) (2008) *The Early Years Foundation Stage: statutory guidance*. London: DCSF.

Department for Children, Schools and Families (DCSF) (2009) *The protection of children in England: a progress report*. London: The Stationery Office. Crown Copyright.

Department for Education (DfE) (2012) *Early Years Foundation Stage Framework*. London: DfE.

Department for Education (2013) *The Children and Families Bill*. London: DfE.

Department for Education (2014a) *Statutory Framework for the Early Years Curriculum*. London: DfE.

Department for Education (2014b) *The National Curriculum Framework for Key Stage 1–4*. London: DfE.

Department for Education and Department of Health (DoH) (2015) *Special educational needs and disability: statutory guidance*. London: DfE and DoH.

Department for Education and Science (DES) (1978) *Special educational needs: report of the committee of enquiry into the education of handicapped children and young people: the Warnock report*. London: HMSO.

Department for Education and Science (1990) *Starting with quality: the Rumbold report*. London: HMSO.

Department for Education and Skills (DfES) (2004a) *Every child matters: change for children*. Ref. DfES 1081/2004. London: DfES.

Department for Education and Skills (2004b) *The Effective Provision of Pre-school Education Project: final report. A longitudinal study: 1997–2004*. Nottingham: DfES.

Department for Education and Skills (2006) *The Rose Review: an independent review of the teaching of early reading*. London: DfES.

Department for Education and Skills (2007) *Practice guidance for the early years foundation stage*. Nottingham: DfES.

Devarakonda, C. (2013) *Diversity and inclusion in early childhood: an introduction*. London: Sage.

Devlin, K. (2003) *Mathematics: the science of patterns*. New York: First Owl Books.

Dockett, S. (2011) 'The challenge of play', in S. Rogers (ed.) *Rethinking play and pedagogy in early childhood education*. London: Routledge.

Donaldson, M. (1986) *Children's minds* (2nd edn). London: HarperCollins.

Draper, L. and Duffy, B. (2010) 'Working with parents', in C. Cable, L. Miller and G. Goodliff (eds) *Working with children in the early years* (2nd edn). Abingdon: Routledge.

Drummond, M.J. (2008) 'Assessment and values: a close and necessary relationship', in S. Swafield (ed.) *Unlocking Assessment*. London: Routledge.

Duffy, B. (2006) *Supporting creativity and imagination in the early years* (2nd edn). Maidenhead: Open University Press.

Duffy, B. and Marshall, J. (2007) 'Leadership in multi-agency working', in I. Siraj-Blatchford, K. Clarke and M. Needham (eds) *The team around the child*. London: Trentham Books.

Duhn, I. (2011) 'Towards professionalism/s', in L. Miller and C. Cable (eds) *Professionalism, leadership and management in the early years*. London: Sage.

Dukes, C. and Smith, M. (2014) *Provision and progress for two year olds*. London: Sage.

Dye, V. (2011) 'Reflection, reflection, reflection, I'm thinking all the time, why do I need a theory or model of reflection?', in D. McGregor and L. Cartwright (eds) *Developing reflective practice*. Maidenhead: Open University Press.

Earley, P. and Porritt, V. (eds) (2009) *Effective practices in continuing professional development: lessons from schools*. London: Institute of Education: University of London.

Education Scotland (2012) *Transforming lives through learning*. Livingston: Education Scotland.

Feasey, R. and Still, M. (2010) 'Science and ICT', in L. Miller, C. Cable and G. Goodliff (eds) *Supporting children's learning in the early years*. Maidenhead: Open University Press.

Field, F. (2010) *The foundation years: preventing poor children becoming poor adults*. London: Her Majesty's Government.

Fisher, J. (2008) *Starting from the child* (3rd edn). Maidenhead: Open University Press.

Fitzgerald, D. (2004) *Parent Partnerships in the Early Years*. London: Continuum.

Flewitt, R. (2008) 'Multimodal literacies', in J. Marsh and E. Hallet (eds) *Desirable literacies*. London: Sage.

Flouri, E. and Buchanan, A. (2004) 'Early father's and mother's involvement and child's later educational outcomes', *Journal of Educational Psychology*, 74 (2) 141–53.

Foot, H., Howe, C., Cheyne, B., Terras, B. and Rattray, C. (2002) 'Parental participation and partnership in preschool provision', *International Journal of Early Years Education*, 10 (1) 5–19.

Forbes, A. and McCloughan, G. (2010) 'Increasing student participation in primary schools: the MYScience initiative', *Teaching Science: the Journal of the Australian Science Teachers Association*, 56 (2) 24–30.

Foundation Degree Forward (FDF) (2005) *Work-based learning: briefing for learning providers*. Lichfield: FDF.

Friedman, R. (2007) 'Professionalism in the early years', in M. Wild and H. Mitchell (eds) *Early childhood studies: a reflective reader*. Exeter: Learning Matters.

Fumoto, H., Robson, S., Greenfield, S. and Hargreaves, D. (2012) *Young children's creative thinking*. London: Sage.

Galton, M. (2000) *Integrating theory and practice*. Paper presented at TLRP conference, Leicester, 1 November.

Gascoyne, S. (2012) *Treasure baskets and beyond*. Maidenhead: Open University Press.

Ghate, D. and Hazel, N. (2001) *Parenting in poor environments: stress, support and coping*. London: Policy Research Bureau.

Giddens, A. (1984) *The constitution of society: outline of the theory of structuration*. Cambridge: Policy Press.

Gillen, J. and Hall, N. (2003) 'The emergence of early childhood literacy', in N. Hall, J. Larson and J. Marsh (eds) *Handbook of early childhood literacy*. London: Sage.

Goldschmied, E. (1987) *Infants at work* (training video). London: National Children's Bureau (NCB).

Goldschmied, E. and Hughes, A. (1986) *Infants at work: babies of 6–9 months exploring everyday objects* (training video). London: NCB.

Goldschmied, E. and Jackson, S. (2004) *People under three*. London: Routledge.

Goleman, D. (2002) *Primal leadership: learning to lead with emotional intelligence*. Boston, MA: Harvard Business School.

Gray, C. and Macblain, S. (2012) *Learning theories in early childhood*. London: Sage.

Guille, D. and Lucas, N. (1999) 'Rethinking the initial teacher education and professional development in further education: towards the learning professional', in A. Green and N. Lucas (eds) *FE and lifelong learning: realigning the sector for the twenty-first century*. London: Bedford Way Papers, Institute of Education.

Hadfield, M., Jopling, M., Waller, T. and Emira, M. (2011) Longitudinal study of early years professional status: interim report. March, University of Wolverhampton.

Hager, P. (2011) 'Theories of workplace learning', in M. Malloch, L. Cairns, K. Evans and B.N. O'Conner (eds) *The international handbook of workplace learning: theory, research, practice and issues*. London: Sage.

Hall, E. (2010) 'Identity and young children's drawings: power, agency, control and transformation', in, P. Broadhead, J. Howard and E. Wood (eds) *Play and learning*. London: Sage.

Hall, N. (1987) *The emergence of literacy*. London: Hodder & Stoughton.

Hall, N. (1999) 'Young children, play and literacy: engagement in realistic uses of literacy', in J. Marsh and E. Hallet (eds) *Desirable literacies: approaches to language and literacy in the early years*. London: Sage.

Hall, N., Larson, J. and Marsh, J. (eds) (2003) *Handbook of Early Childhood Literacy*. London: Sage.

Hallet, E. (1990) *Children as independent writers*. Sheffield: Sheffield Early Years Literacy Association.

Hallet, E. (2005) The implementation of Every Child Matters. Derby: University of Derby. Unpublished research.

Hallet, E. (2008) 'Signs and symbols: children's engagement in environmental print', in J. Marsh and E. Hallet (eds) *Desirable literacies: approaches to language and literacy in the early years* (2nd edn). London: Sage.

Hallet, E. (2009) An investigation into foundation degree graduates' experiences of an early years sector-endorsed foundation degree: implications for practice. Unpublished EdD thesis, University of Derby.

Hallet, E. (2011) The early years curriculum. Unpublished lecture. London: Institute of Education.

Hallet, E. (2012) Working with young children. Unpublished lecture. London: Institute of Education.

Hallet, E. (2013) *The reflective early years practitioner*. London: Sage.

Hallet, E. (2014) *Leadership of learning in early years practice*. London: IOE Press.

Hallet, E. (2015) Poem: Are the children *just playing* today? In *Early Years Practice*.

Hallet, E. and Cortvriend, V. (2008) 'Playing', in I. MacLeod-Brudenell and J. Kay (eds) *Advanced early years*. Harlow: Pearson Educational.

Hallet, E. and Roberts-Holmes, G. (2010) *Research into the contribution of the EYPS role to quality improvement strategies in Gloucestershire: final report*. London: Institute of Education.

Harris, P. (2000) *The work of imagination*. Oxford: Blackwell.

Harrison, J. (2008) 'Professional development and the reflective practitioner', in S. Dymoke and J. Harrison (eds) *Reflective teaching and learning*. London: Sage.

Hendry, H. (2012) 'Diversity in the early years', in P. Beckley (ed.) *Learning in the early years*. London: Sage.

Hevey, D. and Miller, L. (2000) 'Reconceptualising policy making in the early years', in L. Miller and D. Hevey (eds) *Policy issues in the early years*. London: Sage.

Holland, R. (2010) 'What's it all about? How introducing heuristic play has affected provision for under-threes in one day nursery', in C. Cable, L. Miller and G. Goodliff (eds) *Working with children in the early years*. Maidenhead: Open University Press.

Hoskins, E. (2015) 'Play-based science', in M. Dunne and A. Peacock (eds) *Primary science: a guide to teaching practice* (2nd edn). London: Sage.

Howard, J. (2014) 'Play and development in early childhood', in T. Maynard and S. Powell (eds) *An introduction to early childhood studies*. London: Sage.

Hurst, V. and Joseph, J. (2010) 'Parents and practitioners', in C. Cable, L. Miller and G. Goodliff (eds) *Working with children in the early years* (2nd edn). Abingdon: Routledge.

Hutt, J., Tyler, S., Hutt, C. and Cristopherson, H. (1989) *Play, exploration and learning*. London: Routledge.

Jackson, D. and Needham, M. (2014) *Engaging parents in early years settings*. London: Sage.

James, J.H. (2010) 'Teachers as mothers in the elementary classroom: negotiating the needs of the self and other', *Gender and Education*, 22 (5) 521–34.

Jarvis, P., Newman, S., Holland, W. and George, J. (2012) *Research in the early years*. Harlow: Pearson.

Johnston, J. (2005) *Early explorations in science* (2nd edn). Maidenhead: Open University Press.

Johnston, J. (2012) 'Enabling environments', in M. Dunne and A. Peacock (eds) *Primary science: a guide to teaching practice* (2nd edn). London: Sage.

Jones, P. (2009) *Rethinking childhood*. London: Continuum.

Jones, P. (2012) Rethinking early childhood. MA Early Years Education Programme, unpublished lecture. Universtity College London: Institute of Education.

Jones, C. and Pound, L. (2008) *Leadership and management in the early years*. Maidenhead: Open University Press.

Jones, P. and Walker, G. (eds) (2011) *Children's rights in practice*. London: Sage.

Kagan, S.L. and Hallmark, L.G. (2001) 'Cultivating leadership in early care and education', *Childcare Information Exchange*, 140: 7–10.

Kanefsky, J. (2001) 'Research impact and the ESRC teaching and learning research programme', Paper presented at BERA conference, University of Leeds, September.

Kanter, D.E., Honwad, S., Adams, J.D. and Fernandez, A. (2011) 'Guiding play for science and learning in middle school', *Children, youth and environments*, 21 (2) 360–82.

Katz, L. and Chard, S. (2000) *Engaging children's minds* (2nd edn). Stamford, CT: Ablex Publishing.

Kay, J. (2002) *Teaching assistant's handbook*. London: Continuum.

Killion, J. and Todnem, G. (1991) 'A process for personal theory building', *Journal of Educational Leadership*, 48: 14–16.

Knight, S. (2009) *Forest schools and outdoor learning* (2nd edn). London: Sage.

Knight, S. (ed.) (2013) *International perspectives on forest school*. London: Sage.

Knight, T., Tennant, R., Dillon, L. and Weddell, E. (2006) *National centre for social research evaluation of the early years sector-endorsed foundation degree: a qualitative study of students' views and experiences*. Research Brief No. RB751, April. London: DfES.

Knowles, G. (2009) *Ensuring every child matters*. London: Sage.

Kolb, D. (1984) *Experiential learning: experience as the source of learning and development*. Englewood Cliffs, NJ: Prentice Hall.

Kolbe, U. (2000) 'Seeing beyond marks and forms: appreciating children's visual thinking', in W. Schiller (ed.) *Thinking through the arts*. Amsterdam: Harwood Academic Publisher.

Lave, J. and Wenger, E. (1991) *Situated learning: legitimate peripheral participation*. Cambridge: Cambridge University Press.

Lee, N. (2001) *Childhood and society: growing up in an age of uncertainty*. Maidenhead: Open University Press.

Lee, W., Carr, M., Soutar, B. and Mitchell, L. (2013) *Understanding the Te Whariki approach*. Abingdon: Routledge.

Leeson, C. (2010) 'In praise of reflective practice', in R. Parker-Rees, C. Leeson, J. Willan and J. Savage (eds) *Early childhood studies* (2nd edn). Exeter: Learning Matters.

Lehrer, J.S. (2013) 'Accompanying early childhood professional reflection in Quebec: a case study', *Early Years*, 33 (2) 186–200.

Lindon, J. (2010) *The key person approach: positive relationships in the early years*. London: Practical Pre-school Books.

Lipman, M. (2003) *Thinking in education*. Cambridge: Cambridge University Press.

Lord Laming (2003) *The Victoria Climbié Inquiry: report of an inquiry by Lord Laming* (2003) London: The Stationery Office. Crown Copyright.

Luff, P. (2014a) 'Necessary paperwork: observation and assessment in the Early Years Foundation Stage', in J. Moyles, J. Payler, and J. Georgeson (eds) *Early years foundations: critical issues* (2nd edn). Maidenhead: Open University Press.

Luff, P. (2014b) 'Play and creativity', in T. Waller and G. Davis (eds) *An introduction to early childhood* (3rd edn). London: Sage.

Lumby, J. and Coleman, M. (2007) *Leadership and diversity: challenging theory and practice in education*. London: Sage.

McDowall Clark, R. and Murray, J. (2012) *Reconceptualising leadership in the early years*. Maidenhead: Open University Press.

McGuinness, C. (1999) *From thinking skills to thinking classrooms*. Research Report No. 115. London: DfEE.

McNiff, J. (2014) 'Foreword', in R. Walker and C. Solvason (eds) *Success with your early years research project*. London: Sage.

Makin, L. and Jones Diaz, C. (2004) *Literacies in early childhood: challenging views, challenging practice*. Sydney: MacLennan & Petty.

Malaguzzi, L. (1996) *The hundred languages of children: catalogue of exhibition*. Reggio Children. Reggio Emilia, Italy.

Manning, K. and Sharp, A. (1977) *Structuring play in the early years*. London: Ward Locke Educational.

Manning-Morton, J. and Thorp, M. (2010) 'Children from birth to three playing, growing and learning through moving and doing', in L. Miller, C. Cable and G. Goodliff (eds) *Supporting children's learning in the early years* (2nd edn). Maidenhead: Open University Press.

Marsh, J. (2014) 'Childhood in digital age', in T. Maynard and S. Powell (eds) *Early childhood studies* (3rd edn). London: Sage.

Marsick, V.J. and Watkins, K.E. (1999) *Learning organisations*. London: Gower.

Mathers, S., Ranns, H., Karemaker, A., Moody, A., Sylva, K., Graham, J. and Siraj-Blatchford, I. (2011) *Evaluation of the graduate leader fund*. Research Report No. DfE-RR144. London: DfEE.

Maynard, T. and Chicken, S. (2012) 'Exploring Reggio Emilia in a Welsh context', in L. Miller, R. Drury and C. Cable (eds) *Extending professional practice in the early years*. Maidenhead: Open University Press.

Maynard, T. and Powell, S. (eds) (2014) *Early childhood studies* (3rd edn). London: Sage.

Merchant, G. (2008) 'Early reading development', in J. Marsh and E. Hallet (2008) (eds) *Desirable literacies: approaches to language and literacy in the early years*. (2nd edn) London: Sage.

Miller, L. (2010) 'Introduction', in L. Miller, C. Cable and G. Goodliff (eds) *Supporting children's learning in the early years*. Abingdon: Routledge.

Miller, L. and Cable, C. (2008) *Professionalism in the early years*. Abingdon: Hodder Education.

Miller, L. and Cable, C. (eds) (2011) *Professionalization, leadership and management in the early years*. London: Sage.

Montague-Smith, A. and Price, A.J. (2012) *Mathematics in early years education* (3rd edn). London: Routledge.

Moon, J. (2006) *A handbook of reflective and experimental learning*. London: Routledge.

Moss, P. (2003) *Beyond caring: the case for reforming the childcare and early years workforce*. Facing the Future policy paper: London: Daycare Trust.

Moss, P. (2008) 'The democratic and reflective professional: rethinking and reforming the early years workforce', in L. Miller and C. Cable (eds) *Professionalism in the early years*. London: Hodder & Stoughton.

Moss, P. (2011) 'Foreword', in A. Paige-Smith and A. Craft (eds) *Developing reflective practice in the early years* (2nd edn). London: Hodder & Stoughton.

Moss, P. and Petrie, P. (2002) *From children's services to children's spaces*. London: RoutledgeFalmer.

Moyles, J. (2001) 'Passion, paradox and professionalism in early years education', *International Journal for Early Years Education*, 21 (2) 81–95.

Moyles, J. (2006) *Effective leadership and management in the early years*. Maidenhead: Open University Press.

Moyles, J. (2010) *The Excellence of Play* (3rd edn). Berkshire: Open University Press.

Moyles, J. (2010a) 'The powerful means of learning in the early years', in S. Smidt (ed.) *Key issues in early years education* (2nd edn). London: Routledge.

Moyles, J. (2010b) 'Play: the powerful means of learning in the early years', in S. Smidt (ed.) *Key issues in early years education* (2nd edn). London: Routledge. pp. 23–31.

Moyles, J. (2010c) 'Forward', in P. Broadhead, J. Howard and E. Wood (eds) *Play and learning*. London: Sage.

Moylett, H. (2014) 'Observing children to improve practice', in T. Maynard and S. Powell (eds) *Early childhood studies* (3rd edn). London: Sage.

Mukherji, P. and Albon, D. (2015) *Research methods in early childhood: an introductory guide* (2nd edn). London: Sage.

Munro, E. (2010) *Munro review of child protection*. Ref. DfE 00548–2010. London: DfE.

Munton, A.G., Mooney, A. and Rowland, L. (1995) 'Deconstructing quality: a conceptual framework for the new paradigm in daycare provision for the under eights', *Early Childhood Development and Care*, 114 (1) 11–23.

National Advisory Committee on Creative and Cultural Education (NACCCE) (1999) *All our futures: creativity, culture and education*. London: DfEE.

National College for School Leadership (NCSL) (2008) *Realizing leadership: children's centre leaders in action, the impact of NPQICL on children's centre leaders and their practice*. Nottingham: NCSL.

National College for Teaching & Leadership (NCTL) (2013) *Teachers' Standards (Early Years): From September 2013*, July. Ref. NCTL-00108–2013. Available at: www.gov.uk/government/uploads/system/uploads/attachment_data/file/211646/Early_Years_Teachers__Standards.pdf (accessed February 2015).

National College for Teaching & Leadership (NCTL) (2014) NPQICL provider's meeting: early years update, 24 January. Nottingham: NCTL. Unpublished.

Nelson, A. (2011) 'Foreword', in C. Aubrey, *Leading and managing in the early years* (2nd edn). London: Sage.

Neumann, M.E. (2014) 'An examination of touch-screen tablets and emergent literacy in Australian pre-school children', *Australian Journal of Education*, 58–109.

New Zealand Ministry of Education (1995) *Te Whariki: early childhood curriculum*. Wellington: Learning Media.

Nolan, A. and Nuttall, J. (eds) (2013) Special Issue: Integrated children's services: re-thinking research, policy and practice. *Early Years*, 33 (4).

Nutbrown, C. (2012) *Foundations for quality: an independent review of early education and childcare qualifications*. London: DfE.

Nutbrown, C. (2011) *Key concepts in early childhood education and care* (2nd edn). London: Sage.

Nutbrown, C. and Page, J. (2008) *Working with babies and children*. London: Sage.

Nutbrown, C., Clough, P. and Atherton, F. (2013) *Inclusion in the early years* (2nd edn). London: Sage.

Nutbrown, C., Hannon, P. and Morgan, A. (2005) *Early literacy work with families: policy, practice and research*. London: Sage.

Nutkins, S., McDonald, C. and Stephen, M. (2013) *Early childhood education and care*. London: Sage.

Nutley, S., Morton, S., Jung, T. and Boaz, A. (2010) 'Evidence and policy in six European countries: diverse approaches and common challenges', *Evidence and Policy*, 6 (2) 131–44.

O'Conner, A. (2013) *Understanding transitions in the early years: supporting change through attachment and resilience*. Abingdon: Routledge.

Ofsted (2000) *Evaluating educational inclusion*. London: Ofsted.

Organisation for Economic Co-operation and Development (OECD) (2001) *Starting strong I: early childhood education and care*. Paris: OECD.

Organisation for Economic Co-operation and Development (OECD) (2006) *Starting strong II: early childhood education and care*. Paris: OECD.

Osgood, J. (2006) 'Professionalism and performativity: the feminist challenge facing early years practitioners', *Early Years*, 26 (2) 187–99.

Osgood, J. (2010) 'Reconstructing professionalism in ECEC: the case for the "critically reflective emotional professional"', *Early Years*, 30 (2) 119–33.

Osgood, J. (2011) 'Contested constructions of professionalism within the nursery', in L. Miller and C. Cable (eds) *Professionalism, leadership and management in the early years*. London: Sage.

Osgood, J. (2012) *Narratives from the nursery: negotiating professional identities in early childhood*. London: Routledge.

Paige-Smith, A. and Craft, A. (2011) *Developing your early years practice* (3rd edn). London: Sage.

Parker-Rees, R. (2010) 'Active playing and learning', in R. Parker-Rees, C. Leeson, C.J. Willan and J. Savage (eds) *Early childhood studies* (3rd edn). Exeter: Learning Matters.

Pascal, C. and Bertram, T. (2014) 'Transformative dialogues: the impact of participatory research on practice', in A. Clark, R. Flewitt, M. Hammersley and M. Robb (eds) *Understanding research with children and young people*. London: Sage.

Peacock, A. and Dunne, M. (2015) 'Why is science so hard to teach?', in M. Dunne and A. Peacock (eds) *Primary science: a guide to teaching practice* (2nd edn). London: Sage.

Peeters, J. (2007) 'Including men in early childhood education: insights from the European perspective', *NZ Research in Early Childhood Education*, 10: 15–24.

Pen Green (2012) *Early years teaching centres' progress report 2012*. Corby: Pen Green Research Centre.

Pianta, R. and Cox, M. (eds) (1999) *The transition to kindergarten*. Baltimore, MD: Paul Brookes.

Picchio, M., Giandomenico, I.B. and Musatti, T. (2014) 'The use of documentation in a participatory system of evaluation', *Early Years*, 34 (2) 133–45.

Platt, D. (2014) 'Child welfare and protection', in T. Maynard, and S. Powell (eds) *Early childhood studies*. (3rd edn). London: Sage.

Pollard, A., Collins, J., Simco, N., Swaffield, S., Warin, J. and Warwick, P. (2002) *Reflective teaching: effective and evidence informed professional practice*. London: Continuum.

Potter, E.F. and Edens, K.M. (2001) 'Children's motivational beliefs about art', Paper presented at the annual meeting of the American Educational Research Association, Seattle, WA, 10–14 April.

Pound, L. (2001) *Supporting mathematical development*. Maidenhead: Open University Press.

Pound, L. (2014) 'Playing, learning and developing', in J. Moyles, J. Payler and J. Georgeson (eds) *Early years foundations: critical issues*. Maidenhead: Open University Press.

Pramling, N. and Pramling-Samuelsson, I. (2001) 'It's a floating cause "there is a hole": a young child's experience of natural science', *Early Years*, 21 (2) 139–49.

Prout, A. (2005) *The future of childhood*. London: RoutledgeFalmer.

Pugh, G. (2010) 'Foreword', in K. Sylva, E. Melhuish, P. Sammons, I. Siraj-Blatchford, and B. Taggart, *Early childhood matters*. London: Sage.

Quinton, D. (2004) *Supporting parents: messages from research*. London: Jessica Kingsley.

Raelin, J. (2003) *Creating leaderful organisations*. San Francisco, CA: Berrett-Koehler.

Rawlings, A. (2008) *Studying early years: a guide to work-based learning*. Maidenhead: Open University Press.

Reardon, D. (2009) *Achieving early years professional status*. London: Sage.

Reed, M. and Murphy, A. (2012) 'Parents and practitioners: improving quality', in M. Reed and N. Canning (eds) *Implementing quality improvement and change in the early years*. London: Sage.

Reid, J. and Burton, S. (eds) (2014) *Safeguarding and protecting children in the early years*. Abingdon: Routledge.

Rhodes, H. (2008) 'Love matters: family and parenting', Paper presented at Early Intervention International Conference, Nottingham.

Rinaldi, C. (2005) *Dialogue with Reggio Emilia: listening, researching and learning*. Abingdon: Routledge.

Robb, M. (2014) 'Disseminating research: shaping the conversation', in A. Clark, R. Flewitt, M. Hammersley and M. Robb (eds) *Understanding research with children and young people*. London: Sage.

Roberts-Holmes, G. (2009) 'Inclusive policy and practice', in T. Maynard and N. Thomas (eds) *An introduction to early childhood studies* (2nd edn). London: Sage.

Roberts-Holmes, G. (2014) *Doing your early years research project* (3rd edn). London: Sage.

Robins, A. (ed.) (2006) *Mentoring in the early years*. London: Paul Chapman Publishing.

Rodd, J. (2013) *Leadership in early childhood: the pathway to professionalism* (3rd edn). Maidenhead: Open University Press.

Rogers, S. (2000) Play in school: a qualitative study of teacher perspectives. Unpublished PhD, University of Reading.

Rogers, S. (2011) 'Play and pedagogy: a conflict of interests', in S. Rogers (ed.) *Rethinking play and pedagogy in early childhood education*. London: Routledge.

Rogers, S. (2014) 'Enabling pedagogy: meanings and practices', in J. Moyles, J. Payler and J. Georgeson (eds) *Early years foundations: critical issues*. Maidenhead: Open University Press.

Rogers, S. and Evans, J. (2008) *Inside role-play in early childhood*. London: Routledge.

Ruch, G. (2007) 'Reflective practice in contemporary child-care social work: the role of containment', *The British Journal of Social Work*, 37 (4) 659–80.

Runco, M.A. (2003) *Creativity: theories and themes – research, development, and practice*. New York: Academic Press.

Ruxton, S. (2014) 'Achieving policy impact', in A. Clark, R. Flewitt, M. Hammersley and M. Robb (eds) *Understanding research with children and young people*. London: Sage.

Sammons, P. (2010) 'Does pre-school make a difference? Identifying the impact of pre-school on children's cognitive and social behavioural development at different stages', in K. Sylva, E. Melhuish, P. Sammons, I. Siraj-Blatchford and B. Taggart (eds) *Early childhood matters*. London: Sage.

Schaffer, H.R. (2004) 'Using language', in *Introducing child psychology*. Oxford: Blackwell.

Schon, D.A. (1983) *The reflective practitioner*. Aldershot: Aldgate.

Schon, D.A. (1987) *Educating the reflective practitioner*. San Francisco, CA: Jossey-Bass.

Scottish Government (2008) *Early years framework*. Edinburgh: The Scottish Government.

Selbie, P. and Wickett, K. (2010) 'Providing an enabling environment', in R. Parker-Rees, C. Leeson, J. Willan and J. Savage (eds) *Early childhood studies* (3rd edn). Exeter: Learning Matters.

Shirley, I. (2010) 'Exploring the great outdoors', in C. Cable, L. Miller and G. Goodliff (eds) *Working with children in the early years*. Maidenhead: Open University Press.

Sightlines (1996) *Reggio Emilia* (video). Newcastle on Tyne: Sightlines.

Siraj, I. (2014) *Children who have early education get better GCSE results*. London: Institute of Education blog (accessed November 2014).

Siraj, I. and Hallet, E. (2012) National standards for leadership of Sure Start children's centre services: draft revised standards for consultation. London: Institute of Education/Nottingham: NCTL. Unpublished.

Siraj, I. and Hallet, E. (2014) *Effective and caring leadership in early years practice*. London: Sage.

Siraj, I., Kingston, D. and Melhuish, E. (2015) *Assessing quality in early childhood education and care: sustained shared thinking and emotional well-being (SSTEW) scale for 2–5-year-olds provision*. Stoke-on-Trent: Trentham Books.

Siraj-Blatchford, I. (2007) 'Creativity, communication and collaboration: the identification of pedagogic progression in sustained shared thinking', *Asia-Pacific Journal of Research in Early Childhood Education*, 1 (2) 3–23.

Siraj-Blatchford, I. (2010a) Early childhood education: MA lecture. London: Institute of Education. Unpublished.

Siraj-Blatchford, I. (2010b) 'How working class children succeed', *British Educational Research Journal*, 36 (3) 463–82.

Siraj-Blatchford, I. (2014) 'Early childhood education (ECE)', in T. Maynard and N. Thomas (eds) *An introduction to early childhood studies* (3rd edn). London: Sage.

Siraj-Blatchford, I. and Hallet, E. (2012) Draft national standards for leadership of Sure Start children's centre services: for consultation. Nottingham: NCTL. Unpublished.

Siraj-Blatchford, J. and MacLeod-Brudenell, I. (1999) *Supporting science design and technology in early years*. Maidenhead: Open University Press.

Siraj-Blatchford, I. and Manni, L. (2007) *Effective leadership in the early years sector (ELEYS study)*. London: Institute of Education.

Siraj-Blatchford, I. and Sylva, K. (2004) 'Researching pedagogy in English pre-schools', *British Educational Research Journal*, 30 (5) 713–30.

Siraj-Blatchford, I. Clarke, K. and Needham, M. (2007) (eds) *The team around the child: multi-agency working*. Stoke-on-Trent: Trentham Books.

Smith, F. (1971) *Understanding reading: a psycholinguistic analysis of reading and learning to read*. London: Hodder and Stoughton.

Smith, P.K., Cowie, H. and Blades, M. (2003) *Understanding children's development.* (4th edn) Oxford: Blackwell.

Solley, K. (2003) 'What do early childhood leaders do to maintain and enhance the significance of the early years?' Paper presented at the Institute of Education, London, 22 May.

Springate, D. and Foley, P. (2008) 'Play matters', in J. Collins and P. Foley (eds) *Promoting children's well-being.* Bristol: Policy Press.

Stephens, C. (2006) *Perspectives of early years education from a review of international literature.* Edinburgh: Scottish Executive Education Department.

Sternberg, R.J. (2003) 'Creative thinking in the classroom', *Scandinavian Journal of Educational Research*, 43 (3) 325–38.

Stewart, N. (2011) *How children learn.* London: British Association for Early Childhood Education.

Sullivan, A. and Brown, M. (2014) *Research identifies types of reading that can lead to higher vocabulary.* London: Centre for Longitudinal Studies, Institute of Education.

Sure Start (2002) *Birth to three matters framework.* London: DfES/Sure Start.

Swim, T.J. and Isik-Ercan, Z. (2013) 'Dispositional development as a form of continuous professional development: centre-based reflective practices with teachers of very young children', *Early Years*, 33 (2) 172–85.

Sylva, K. (2010) 'Quality in early childhood settings', in K. Sylva, E. Melhuish, P. Sammons, I. Siraj-Blatchford and B. Taggart (eds) *Early childhood matters.* London: Sage.

Sylva, K., Melhuish, E., Sammons, P. and Siraj-Blatchford, I. (1999) *The Effective Provision of Pre-school Education (EPPE project): a longitudinal study funded by the DfEE 1997–2003* London: Institute of Education.

Sylva, K., Melhuish, E., Sammons, P., Siraj-Blatchford, I. and Taggart, B. (2004) *The Effective Provision of Pre-school Education (EPPE project): final report.* London: DfES/Institute of Education.

Sylva, K., Melhuish, E., Sammons, P., Siraj-Blatchford, I. and Taggart, B. (eds) (2010) *Early childhood matters.* London: Sage.

Sylva, K., Siraj-Blatchford, I. and Taggart, B. (2003) *Assessing quality in the early years: early childhood environmental rating scale extension (ECERS-E).* Stoke-on-Trent: Trentham Books.

Sylva, K., Taggart, B., Melhuish, E., Sammons, P. and Siraj-Blatchford, I. (2007) 'Changing models of research to inform educational policy', *Research Papers in Education*, 22 (2) 155–68.

Sylva, K., Taggart, B., Melhuish, E., Sammons, P. and Siraj, I. (2014) *Effective Pre-school, Primary and Secondary Education (EPPSE) research reports and findings* http://eppe.ioe.ac.uk (accessed July 2015)

Taggart, B. (2010) 'Making a difference: how research can inform policy', in K. Sylva, E. Melhuish, P. Sammons, I. Siraj-Blatchford and B. Taggart (eds) *Early childhood matters*. London: Sage.

Taggart, G. (2011) 'Don't we care? The ethics and emotional labour of early years professionalism', *Early Years*, 31 (1) 85–95.

Taggart, B., Siraj-Blatchford, I., Sylva, K., Melhuish, E. and Sammons, P. (2008) 'Influencing policy through research on early childhood education', *International Journal of Early Childhood Education*, 12 (2) 7–21.

Teather, S. (2010) 'The policy context in the Centre for Educational Outcomes (C4EO)', in *Grasping the nettle: early intervention for children, families and communities*. London: C4EO.

Thomas, N. (2014) 'Sociology of childhood', in P. Mukherji and L. Dryden (eds) *Foundations of early childhood: principles and practice*. London: Sage.

Tickell, C. (2011) *The early years: foundations for life, health and learning*. London: DfE.

Trevarthen, C. and Aitken, K.J. (2001) 'Infant inter-subjectivity: research, theory and clinical applications', *Journal of Child Psychology and Psychiatry*, 42: 3–48.

Trickey, S. and Topping, K.J. (2004) 'Philosophy for children', *Research Papers in Education*, 19 (3) 365–80.

Truss, E. (2013) *More great childcare: raising quality and giving parents more choice*. London: DfE.

Trussler, S. and Robinson, D. (2015) *Inclusive practice in the primary school: a guide for teachers*. London: Sage.

Tsang, N. (2007) 'Reflection as dialogue', *British Journal of Social Work*, 37 (4) 681–94.

Tucker, K. (2014) *Mathematics through play in the early years* (3rd edn). London: Sage.

Turley, C. (2009) 'Fostering reflective practice', in *Radiation Therapist*, 18 (1) 66–8.

United Nations (UN) (1989) *The Convention on the Rights of the Child*. Geneva: UN.

Urban, M. (2010) 'Rethinking professionalism in early childhood: untested feasibilities and critical ecologies', *Contemporary Issues in Early Childhood*, 11 (1) 1–7.

Vincent, C. (1996) *Parents and teachers: power and participation*. London: Falmer Press.

Vygotsky, L.S. (2004) 'Imagination and creativity in early childhood', *Journal of Russian and East European Psychology*, 42 (1) 7–97.

Waller, T. (2009) 'Outdoor play and learning', in T. Waller (ed.) *An introduction to early childhood*. London: Sage.

Waters, J. (2013) 'Talking in wild outdoor spaces: children bringing their interest to their teachers in Wales', in S. Knight (ed.) *International perspectives on forest school*. London: Sage.

Waugh, N. (2013) 'Comment from England', in W. Lee, M. Carr, B. Soutar and L. Mitchell (eds) *Understanding the Te Whariki approach*. Abingdon: Routledge. p. 108.

Welsh Government (2008) *The Foundation Phase*. Wales: The Welsh Government.

Wenger, E. (1998) *Communities of practice, learning, meaning, identity*. New York: Cambridge University Press.

Westwood, J. (2014) 'Childhood in different countries', in T. Maynard and S. Powell (eds) *Early childhood studies* (3rd edn). London: Sage.

Whalley, M. (1999) Women as leaders in early childhood settings: a dialogue in the 1990s. Unpublished PhD thesis, University of Wolverhampton.

Whalley, M. (2007) *Involving parents in their children's learning* (2nd edn). London: Sage.

Whalley, M.E. (2011) 'Leading and managing in the early years', in L. Miller and C. Cable (eds) *Professionalisation, leadership and management in the early years*. London: Sage. pp. 13–28.

Whitebread, D. (2000) 'Teaching children to think, reason, solve problems and be creative', in D. Whitebread (ed.) *The psychology of teaching and learning in the primary school*. London: RoutledgeFalmer.

Whitebread, D. (2012) *Developmental psychology and early childhood education*. London: Sage.

Whitehouse, A. (2014) 'Critical friends: the reflective facilitators', in C. Hayes, J. Daly, M. Duncan, R. Gill and A. Whitehouse (eds) *Developing as a reflective early years professional: a thematic approach*. Northwich: Critical Publishing.

Willow, C. (2014) 'Upholding children's rights in early childhood settings', in P. Mukherji and L. Dryden (eds) *Foundations of early childhood: principles and practice*. London: Sage.

Wilson, R. (2012) *Nature and young children* (2nd edn). London: David Fulton.

Winnicott, D. (1953) 'Transitional objects and transitional phenomena', *International Journal of Psychoanalysis*, 34: 89–97.

Wood, E. (2010) 'Developing integrated pedagogical approaches to play and learning', in P. Broadhead, J. Howard and E. Wood (eds) *Play and learning in the early years*. London: Sage.

Wray, D., Bloom, W. and Hall, N. (1989) *Literacy in action*. London: Falmer Press.

Wright, S. (2010) *Understanding creativity in early childhood*. London: Sage.

Wyse, D. (ed.) (2004) *Childhood studies: an introduction*. Maidenhead: Open University Press.

Young-Loveridge, J.M. (2008) 'Developing young children's mathematical thinking for a knowledge-based economy', Paper given at Pacific Early Childhood Education Research Association (PECERA) 9th Annual Conference, Bangkok, Thailand, 6–9 July.

Index

Added to a page number 'f' denotes a figure and 't' denotes a table.